The Doormat Syndrome

Lynne Namka

Authors Choice Press

San Jose New York Lincoln Shanghai

The Doormat Syndrome

Authors Choice Press
an imprint of iUniverse.com, Inc.

For information address:
iUniverse.com, Inc.
5220 S 16th, Ste. 200
Lincoln, NE 68512
www.iuniverse.com

Originally published by Health Communications

ISBN: 0-595-16060-3

DEDICATION

In gratitude, humility and laughter, this book is dedicated to my mother, Rhea Wickiser, my father, the late Roland Wickiser, and my children, John M. Grimes, Kathy Grimes and Karen Armstrong. It is also dedicated to the memory of my teacher, the most marvelous Virginia Satir.

✺ ACKNOWLEDGMENTS ✺

There are so many women who have been loving sisters to me all of my life and I have learned much from their kindness and generosity. I am indebted to those special women who have served as teachers for me: Marcia White, Gayle Stewart, Carolyn Jefferies and, of course, Virginia Satir. I am also thankful for my university advisors who believed in me at a time in my life when I did not believe in myself: Dr. Laura Jordan and Dr. Herb Morice.

However, it has been the men in my life who have presented me with the most exciting and challenging lessons regarding co-dependency. John Bailey showed me my poetic self. David Wilkinson, in his commentaries at St. Francis of the Foothills Church, encouraged us weekly to live our visions. Don Smith convinced me that I was truly funny. Peter Burnham helped me learn about friendship with men. There is another, who wishes to remain anonymous, who taught me about power, submission and dominance. Jerry Weinberg taught me to be myself and express my true loving nature. To all of the people across my life who hve been part of my process in becoming a strong and loving woman, I am very grateful.

I further want to acknowledge all of the researchers in the fields of psychology and addiction who add to the knowledge base on how to live in freedom. I appreciate the efforts of my editor, Marie Stilkind, and the staff at Health Communications for their contributions in the addiction field.

Thanks go to my dear friend, Peggy Dunlap, who lovingly provided the proofreading.

I would also like to thank Jacob Shloss for his art concepts.

❧ CONTENTS ❧

❧ INTRODUCTION ❧

So you've just been stepped on again! You've found yourself flat on the floor and someone has walked all over you — squashed your face and messed up your clothes. This time, however, it happened with a brand new awareness. You are, after all, a person of the '80s. Somehow you have survived taking care of others, rescuing those who didn't want to be rescued and giving it all away to those who sometimes didn't want it. The new improved version of yourself has a new level of understanding. You may even have a new vocabulary word for your irrational behavior: co-dependency. But it still happened to you again; you let someone take advantage of you.

This book is about relationships — relationships with others, but mostly about a relationship with yourself. If you have ever given to the point of exhaustion, felt dumped on or ripped off, and puzzled to find yourself coming back for more, then you may find yourself in the pages of this book. If you are involved with people who do not appreciate you, then this book is for you. If you have ever identified with T. S. Eliot's J. Alfred Prufrock who measured out his life with coffee spoons, read on!

You may not have done much reading in the area of co-dependency before. If not, this book not only will give you a good idea of what it is, but also will tell you what to do about it. Or you may be knowledgeable about the topic, but still caught up in nonproductive behavior. After reading umpteen books (real heavy books) on co-dependency, you have a new topic in your life to feel guilty about. You should, you know, really **should** give up your co-dependent behavior and get on with it. Enough of this Doormat stuff! That's what a really decent, giving person would do. But somehow knowing about self-defeating behavior just isn't enough. If it were, we would all be perfectly well-adjusted and saintly besides. Now that you've finally got a name for your personal craziness, what in the name of heaven do you do with it? Will the real (fill in your name here) lie down? Or is there a better way?

The Gestalt psychology folk among us do have a point. Sometimes it is not enough just to know about something. Experiential is the word. We human beings have to feel something and experience it on a deep, deep level before we are shook up enough to really get the message of change. Change is a tricky business, after all; it takes a lot to get us off of the inertia of our "duff" and get moving. Sometimes we have to hit bottom before we make the decision to get up off the floor and feel good enough about ourselves to decide we have spent enough of our lives running after other people and not enough time riding roller coasters, or skipping, creating or whatever else turns us on.

People treat you the way you treat yourself. It takes experience and practice to learn something new. And that's what this book is about. Experiencing yourself in new ways so that you can become that new, enlightened version. No heavy stuff. No guilt trips for not doing it right, now that you know what's wrong with you. In this book are experiences from A to Z to help you let go, give up, release and throw away those belief systems. That is the purpose of the exercises. Research shows that writing about your problems can help resolve them. Don't just read the book; do the worksheets. Your beliefs about yourself and how things must be have, up to this point in time, bound you to co-dependency. This book will help you develop the attitude of "No more of this do it to me one more time nonsense." Enough is enough.

So here is a fresh outlook on Doormat behavior. The old Brand X definition of co-dependency was based on the medical model, the disease model and the pathology model. Not so here. The approach in this book is based on a wholeness model developed by Virginia Satir and from the theories of Carl Jung. This approach is the mature version for discriminating viewers who want to feel good about themselves while learning to feel good about themselves.

Co-dependency is a set of unproductive behaviors that have been learned and continue because of poor self-esteem. Negative statements about the self and the accompanying emotions of guilt, denial, anger and anxiety perpetuate the self-defeating behavior. Co-dependency is an addiction to relationships that are dysfunctional in nature. The co-dependent person seeks satisfaction from an external source to make up for the lack that is within. In that sense, it is a spiritual craving to merge in a relationship with someone else. Co-dependent behavior is a search for the spiritual part of one's self.

For the Doormat, there is no fix like the fix of fixing someone who is perceived to be broken. That's the heavy part. Now for the lightness, cheer and happiness part. What has been learned can be unlearned! We are evolving, ever-growing creatures if we but choose to be. Learning about co-dependency is a process of growth and the privilege of moving toward wholeness. Co-dependency is an opportunity to learn an important life lesson of equally valuing the self and others. The process of release from co-dependency is a way to find your balance and to learn to be in touch with your divinity. Recovery from co-dependency is finding the spiritual path that is uniquely yours.

Now you may ask (and quite appropriately so) how do you know so much? I have the very best qualifications — I have been so dumb. Over the years I have engaged in most of the basically stupid Doormat behaviors known to the western world. But I do not suffer from terminal dumbness (although for many years this was a debatable issue). The moment of recognition for me came when I was very ill and Virginia Satir was working with me in front of a group of people. She looked at me while she said to the group, "When you can feel your feelings, you won't have to turn them into body symptoms." Something shattered in me that moment and I started feeling all the blocked up emotions that were within me.

I have learned new belief systems to replace those old Doormat beliefs. In my process of becoming an independent person, I have learned strategies to cope with the stress and tension that used to result in typical Doormat behavior. I have learned to disengage myself from the craziness to form a new identity of myself. I have taught these techniques to others in therapy and workshops, and have had some fun along the way. Using humor has been a major technique for my recovery.

Kahlil Gibran said, "A sense of humor is a sense of proportion. One of the evidences of emotional maturity is the ability to laugh at ourselves." Grown-up children of alcoholics and other dysfunctional families often have difficulty having fun. Part of the recovery process is to learn to laugh and play. Through the course of my life, I have resolved never to understand the gravity of things. As the poet John Bailey put it, "I pursue each feather of foolishness." As we are better able to see our self-limiting actions in a funny light, we can make more mature choices.

Having a sense of humor is also a sign of high self-esteem. Humor is healing. Laughter sets the stage for release. Laughing changes the physiological makeup by releasing chemicals in your brain that are beneficial to the body and strengthen the immune system. We can look at our crazymaking in a humorous way and in doing so release some of the emotional blockage we have picked up along the way.

The thing to do is to begin. The process of learning about yourself and about how to get what you want out of life is an exciting journey. So let's get on with it, experientially, of course. And on the way, remember to be gentle and loving with yourself. Now, on to the process!

❧ ONE ❧

The Making Of
The Doormat

Love one another, but make not a bond of love. Let it rather be a moving sea between the shores of your souls.

Kahlil Gibran
The Prophet

We Are All Recovering Human Beings

Co-dependency is an addiction to dysfunctional love relationships. It results from a need to be whole, an attempt to find connection and completion by getting high off another person. It is an addiction that takes away personal power. It is looking outside the self for worth and relying on external sources for validation. Once you understand it for what it is — simply the search for the inner self and the need to be connected at a deep spiritual level — then its unproductive parts can be addressed and released.

All addictions have a spiritual basis. Addictive behavior stems from spiritual poverty resulting in a pattern of seeking satisfaction from an external source rather than finding it within one's own self. It is a disruption

1

of that inner search that wants to merge with something larger and more complete in order to provide distraction from the pain and stress of daily living. It is the search for connection and oneness, and the urge for transcendence to something greater than we are. The 12-Step programs that have been so successful in helping individuals recover from addictive behavior work because they are based on profound spiritual principles.

Co-dependency is a common coping style of behavior characterized by a preoccupation of meeting the needs of other persons to the point of feeling responsible for them at the expense of yourself. One underlying mechanism in co-dependency is a need to control the behavior of other people to help bring order out of the chaos that one feels. It is playing the crazy caretaking role to the ultimate. The person with Doormat behavior is more concerned about others, and their needs and behaviors to such a degree that their own feeling of self-worth depends on trying to rescue others. The person who experiences the Doormat Syndrome is enmeshed in relationships with people who are caught in addictive behavior, such as chemical dependency, or a work, sexual or power addiction. Doormats become hooked into feeling good by pleasing someone else. But in reality the taking care of, the giving and the pleasing are all attempts to control the attitudes and behaviors of the other person.

Co-dependency is more typically found in women because of the cultural messages of subservience, but it is also found in men. The syndrome can manifest itself in taking care of family members or in the workplace. Even independent, self-assertive individuals who operate well in other spheres of their life can engage in co-dependent behavior in their primary loving relationship. They sacrifice their own personhood and the more they do so, the more the relationship is put in jeopardy because the other person either splits physically or withdraws, unable to deal with the overintrusiveness. The co-dependent brain says, "If I just take care of others enough, feel sorry for myself enough, and pout long enough, then I can be lovable."

But first, here's a word about denial, the hallmark of the co-dependency syndrome. Denial is the major defense mechanism of the addictive personality. It creates emotional numbness to help protect the self. Denial allows for the illusion that you are really in control. If you hear yourself saying, "I'm not like that," "That doesn't apply to me," or "I'm not involved with someone who is addicted to drugs, alcohol, work, power or destructive behavior," look again. It may be that old protector, denial, that doesn't want to look at the painful truth. Denial is that part of yourself that wants to play it safe, not rock the boat and live with the illusion that everything is hunky-dory. Denial is also being dishonest with yourself or having the "Ozzie and Harriet" mind-set that sees everything in sweetness and light. It is just one more learned coping style of behavior that is dysfunctional — if you don't see it, then you don't have to deal with it. In this sense denial is your protector; it is like a friend to you. But it can be a false friend.

There are different types of denial that Doormats manifest. On some level of awareness, the Doormat is aware of the problem but unconsciously chooses one or more of the levels of denial as a coping strategy to deal with the pain surrounding the situation. First, there is denial of the fact. Actual reality is distorted as to what is going on and what the extent of the problem is. The second type of denial concerns the consequence of the co-dependent behavior. The facts are registered but there is a "So what? What's the big deal? That's the way things are," type of attitude. The next type is denial of personal feelings; emotions are numbed to cope with the situation. There is knowledge of the events and an understanding of the outcome, but the person refuses to feel bad and adopts a Pollyanna approach. Another type of denial is refusing to consider the necessary changes in life. The underlying attitude may be, "Yes, it's true and it's getting worse. I feel bad about it, but there is nothing I can do." With this attitude, help or treatment is not sought. The last type of denial is to deny that you are in denial.

Honoring Your Old Friend Denial

Here is an exercise to help you look at what part denial may play in your life: Within you is an inner part that is intuitive, all wise, knowing and readily available to help guide daily choices. It is called Higher Power, the Inner Wisdom, the Wisdom Box, God Self or Highest Self. This is the Power within us to control our own destiny. The antidote to co-dependent behavior is to use this Inner Wisdom to make good decisions and develop a strong sense of who you are. "Not me," you may say, and that may be true. But that "not me" may also be your old friend denial cropping up to preserve the status quo and keep you from looking at that stuck part of your life. One way to determine this is to honor the "not me" as denial, and see if anything shifts, allowing you to see yourself more clearly.

Shut your eyes and breathe deeply as you concentrate on one of the more pertinent characteristics from the Doormat characteristics listed below that you have checked. Ask yourself the question, "How does co-dependent behavior manifest itself in my life?" Wait and listen. If nothing comes up for you, then stop and honor the denial you may be feeling. Thank it for protecting you in the past and give it recognition for taking good care of you. Talk to it as if it were your best friend who has always been there for you. For in truth, this is so. You might even give it a name of its own. Tell the denial that you feel safe enough to gain more information about yourself. Ask it to step aside for a moment while you check out the question about the characteristic again. Remember, you have to first know where you are to know where you are going. Acceptance of the reality of denial is the first step in changing your behavior.

Continue to deep breathe and center yourself. Allow your Inner Wisdom that is all knowing and loving to come forth; ask it to help you in your endeavor in seeking the truth about self-defeating behavior. Affirm that you are ready to hear what you need to learn at this point. Allow a deep longing for truth to permeate your whole being. Ask if there is anything you need to know about your old friend denial. If you become frightened, honor the fear. Label it and remind yourself that it is all right to become frightened when you look at something new. Breathe into the fear and turn it into excitement.

Say to yourself three times, "I allow myself to accept the partial truth about

_____.

I allow myself to hear and experience what is right for me to know. I grant the permission to know what is harmful to me in my life. I am now ready

to learn the whole truth. The truth I can learn about myself is _____

_____."

Make a list of the areas of your life where you have handed your personal power over to another person in order to keep the relationship secure. Determine what aspects of yourself you have given up in order to meet the needs of others.

_____

_____

_____

_____

Thank your Higher Power for the assistance it has given you.

Portrait Of The Doormat Syndrome

Now that denial feels safer, let us look at Doormat behavior. So how do you know you are a Doormat? Other than the fact that you still have mud on your face from the last time you tried to help someone who walked all over you? So here it is, folks: A list of symptoms to fit all seasons. You've heard of the "Rich and Famous"? In life you pay your quarter and you take your choices. What do you see in this list for the scraping and placating that fits for you? But first, take a look in the mirror in Figure 1.

Impending sense of doom
hanging over your head

Bowed head from a lifetime
of allowing yourself to
be squelched

Swiss cheese brain with holes
where the common sense
should be

Hang-dog look of "Nobody
appreciates how hard
I'm trying."

Marshmallows instead of
gray matter in the brain

Nose always out of joint
because you stick it in other
people's business

Limited vocabulary that
consists of "Yes, let me help;
that's all right, and it really
doesn't matter," all the time

Black and blue marks from
being shoved around
all the time

Permanently hunched
shoulders from carrying
others on your back

Piece of limp spaghetti
for a backbone

Thick calluses on your knees
from all that bowing,
groveling and scraping

Tiptoeing about walking on
eggshells trying to keep
the peace

Continuously off balance from bending over backward

Figure 1.1. Do You See Yourself In This Mirror?

Characteristics Of The Doormat Syndrome

_____ Highly developed sensitive nature concerning the needs of others

_____ Overemphasis on being responsible for others to the exclusion of taking responsibility for your own behavior

_____ Enmeshment in a relationship with a chemically dependent personality, disordered or other co-dependent or power needy person

_____ Fear of abandonment from your partner within that dysfunctional relationship resulting in submissive behavior

_____ Tendency to become a victim of recurring physical, sexual or emotional abuse

_____ Addiction to chemical substances and/or disordered love relationships

_____ Pervasive lack of self-esteem resulting in inner beliefs of worthlessness, and a lack of confidence in your own ability

_____ Strong negative emotions of fear, anxiety, depression and guilt

_____ Acceptance of the sick, martyr or victim role

_____ Perfectionistic and unrealistic expectation of the self

_____ Hidden need to control others through manipulating them to do it your way or having them think well of you

_____ Need for seeking validation and gratification from others and not from yourself

_____ Image of the self as having little or no power of choice resulting in a narrowed set of behaviors

_____ Highly developed passive-aggressive behavior style with agreeing and then doing what you want

_____ Pattern of developing stress-related illness

_____ Need for hypervigilant behavior of continually checking out the environment

_____ Need to continually set up situations where others move in to perpetuate the co-dependency

_____ Approach of using giving as a means of feeling safe to ward off underlying fears of rejection

_____ Shutting down emotions and feelings resulting in psychological numbness.

Whew! Those characteristics are enough to render a plowhorse helpless! The hooks of the rescuer are many. It is always higher on the scale to please someone else than oneself. Doormat behavior means putting aside your own opinion, values and needs in order to try to connect with the other person. The bottom line is poor self-esteem. Crazy as it may sound, Doormat behavior is a system of learned coping strategies of trying to feel good about yourself. Whether a person is dependent or co-dependent, the problem is the same — a basic lack of self-love.

How did you do on the checklist? Did reading it make your palms sweaty and nervous? If you are a dyed-in-the-wool Doormat or even have a smidgen of the characteristics, by now you should be experiencing the *"Wow!"* effect. The *"Wow, that is really me* and now I'm ready to do something about it" effect.

Honorable Cause Of The Doormat

What are some of the demented things you choose to do to be true, blue and loyal to the honorable cause of the Doormat? Do you . . .

- End up cooking and cleaning up the entire Thanksgiving and Christmas dinner?
- Run ahead of others so that you can open doors for them?
- Faithfully iron your husband's shorts when you never have time to read a juicy novel?
- Convince your family that you only like the chicken necks and backs?
- Consistently bail out helpless people who are sure to fall on their faces if you are not there?
- Make it up to those poor souls who have been hurt by life's slings and arrows?
- Perpetually go without so that he, she or they can go in style?

Do any of these light up your board and ring your bell? If so, your posture may be on permanent tilt from leaning over backward to. fix it up for someone else. That's fine if your lifetime goal is to be a diagonal line, but hardly a position to successfully run a life.

Getting That PhD In Standing On Your Own Two Feet

The symptoms are the bad news. The good news is that this pattern of learned behavior, which is based on learned belief systems, can be unlearned. We rescuer types can learn to think and act differently. In this sense there is no bad news; there is only learning. We can patch up those holes in the brain where the common sense should be. You can drop out of Doormat School and go on to the University of Standing On Your Own Two Feet.

So how do you learn to stop overdosing on helping others? The first step is to acknowledge your condition. Acknowledge your particular brand of crazy behavior that contributes to unproductive relationships. To acknowledge is to open the doors of denial, letting in the sunshine. And in that first step of opening up, you start the process of mental housecleaning.

There is a fine discrimination to be made between co-dependent behavior and acts that are mature and generous. Healthy individuals can give of themselves in ways that are nonthreatening to the core of who they really are. When boundaries for the protection of the self-identity are set in a healthy way, then giving and responding to others becomes a spontaneous act based on what is right for you at the time and the situation rather than acting out of guilt or anxiety. There is little or no attachment to the outcome because there can be giving out of generosity and joy rather than an unconscious need for manipulation. When you learn to fully define who you are and what is right for you, then it is equally right to say yes or no. Decisions are easier to make because they are made from the open, loving self rather from that protective, manipulative self. As you practice this new art of giving from your true sense of self, you will find it easier to determine the real intent of your behavior.

With these encouraging thoughts in mind, go back through the list of characteristics a second time. That's it; take a deep breath and let your own Inner Wisdom do the walking through the list in a way that is safe for you. Note mentally the characteristics that seem to fit. Also notice those items that upset you greatly; this upset may be denial trying to distract you. Give each item on the list of characteristics the NSMA test — that's N for **None of the Time**, S for **Some of the Time**, M for **Most of the Time** and the zinger, A for **All of the Time**.

We won't do a numerical tally on this. Doormat people aren't particularly good at counting. If we really knew what counted in life, we wouldn't spend so much time in the supergiving mode. Just "intuit" it. Are you or are you not? You'll know. And you will also know to what degree, with whom, how much and all those other things you really can know about yourself when denial is safely tucked away.

Now make a list of your own behaviors that are lopsided.

_____

_____

_____

_____

_____

The Things I Did For "Luv"

Okay, 'fess up and write down all of the crazy, weird things you do for others that aren't really necessary. Get in touch with your acts that leave you feeling uncomfortable and out of sorts. Co-dependent behavior is compulsive and obsessive; there is always a sense of anxiety connected with it. Behind each action is a "should, ought, must or have to" in order to feel good about yourself. If there is an element of rescuing others or doing something for their own good, it probably is co-dependency.

Close your eyes and count backward from seven to one while your mind becomes still and quiet. Breathe deeply and begin to consider what acts you engage in that really bother you. Allow your mind to gently prod you about your actions that are invading your basic sense of integrity. Thank your subconscious mind as each thought surfaces. Don't stop to think about your actions at this time; just list each crazy behavior and allow another to come forth.

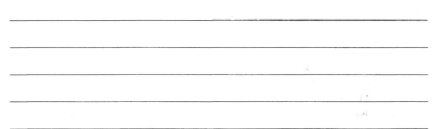

Now you know. Congratulate yourself on taking that first step of acknowledgment. Stop right here and give yourself thanks for recognizing new and important information about yourself. Self recognition and reinforcement for new learning are necessary and potent techniques to bring about change. Now don't get into an argument with those parts of your personality that are self-critical. Just say, "Not now, I'm not going to put myself down; I'm just practicing congratulating myself."

Research Doesn't Get Any More Stirring Than This

Recent research has looked at the type of attachments that children form with their parents in childhood.

Avoidant Attached

The *Avoidant Attached* are those people who have never learned to trust other people or depend on them because their basic needs were not met in childhood by their parents. They tend to have harsh views about their parents. They are cynical about romance and fear intimacy because they do not feel safe depending on anyone but themselves. They go through life swinging back and forth from highs to lows as they try to get those early needs of security met. They always fall short in a relationship because they do not have the underlying security and trust in themselves or others to pull it off.

Anxious And Ambivalent

Another category is the *Anxious and Ambivalent.* These people also go to emotional extremes. They have a strong desire to unite with their partners and demand more closeness than others can safely give. With their excessive need for intimacy, they are often jealous and worry about being left and abandoned. There are mixed reports of parenting styles of the Anxious and Ambivalent.

Securely Attached

The third group is the *Securely Attached.* They have experienced parents who were warm, responsive and loving. They find it easy to get close to other people and have fewer problems with dependence or avoidance in relationships. This group has fewer addictions. They tend to choose partners with whom they can have a mature relationship. "Those that has gets more."

Coping Styles

Virginia Satir, a world-renowned theorist in family systems and therapy, gives a different outlook. She describes coping styles instead of personality types. Coping styles are the ways we deal with the world. They are learned behavior patterns to deal with stress. The coping styles are ways that we learned to protect ourselves and attempt to get love. The methods of coping that we learned when we were much smaller than our parents are often the same ways we deal with current issues at hand. They often tend to be unproductive because they are learned early in life when we don't have much experience or mature problem-solving skills. This learned style of behavior model is a different ballgame than the disease model or fixed characteristics of the personality as it offers hope for change.

A Tiny Stranger In A Strange, Strange Land

Now let's see how it all begins. The tiny baby is perfect. All the baby wants to do is get its own needs met and express itself. It does not know fault and self-criticism. Erik Erikson, a theorist about the normal developmental stages of life, said that the task of infants is to learn to trust their world. Young children need to learn that those around them are consistent and loving. If they feel a threat to themselves or to those around them, they may feel the danger of being abandoned. If the basic needs of warmth, food, shelter, safety and being loved are not met, children go through life trying to find them.

When we follow our adult pain to its roots, we generally find a wounded child. Within each person who is caught up in co-dependency, there is a little child who still is trying to make some sense out of the pain and confusion. Wounded children seek strategies to deal with hurt, pain and rejection that they feel and that others are experiencing in the family. The only strategies that little children had available were extremely restricted, being based on that one- two- or three-year-old mind and its understanding of the world.

Some children love their parents so much that they adopt or take on crazy behavior to protect the parents. They take on an "I'll take care of you" style of behavior if the parents can't take care of themselves. They may take on the parents' shame, fear or depression. If the parents cannot love themselves in some way and are caught up in a destructive pattern with alcohol, drugs, illness or an unhappy relationship, the craziness jumps to the children. It jumps to "I'll make it better for you, Mom or Dad." Or "I'll be perfect for you." Young children take on the grown-up role. This role reversal that is learned at the parents' knee is often at the bottom of co-dependency. Co-dependency is learned behavior that is reinforced by those in authority when children please the parents. It's learned by going to Doormat School.

The pattern happens when the parent has become helpless through alcohol, drugs, mental or physical illness or a lifetime of irresponsibility. To survive children may take over the household at an early age. Another common pattern is learning co-dependency directly by seeing Doormat behavior modeled by parents who overextend themselves by helping others. The common denominator in all of these dysfunctional parenting styles is that children end up playing the role of the adult and in doing so do not experience the normal childhood task of emotionally separating from the parent. Some families are a hotbed of co-dependents inbreeding and perpetuating their own kind. In every family there is sure to be one or two members who thrive on the soap opera mentality of adding spice to life by finding others to rescue.

Children feel abandoned by their parent who is not there psychologically or physically for them in their time of need. But the real abandonment that can take place is for children to give up themselves. A part of the child dies so that the parent can live. At some point children make a decision to take care of one or more people in the family. Children abandon their little child part and become miniature adults feeling responsible for the care of those around them.

Co-dependency becomes a power issue based on trying to cope with the pain that is in the family. It is more often found in girls, although it is also prevalent in some boys. It appears in those children in the family who are more sensitive in nature. Children who are in a subordinate position in the family learn about meeting the needs of those who are dominant. Co-dependent children learn to reject their own internal values and validate themselves by what others think and say. Feeling good inside becomes tied to pleasing others. They grow up believing that unless they are taking care of someone else, they are not valued.

Critical and negative messages from the parents to the children contribute to feelings of never being good enough. There is no seduction like that of being a good little girl or boy, the martyr or the generous giver. Those cumulative pats on the head while growing up for giving and taking care of someone else have had a weighty effect. Positive messages, such as "Be a good little girl or boy," may also contribute to poor self-esteem if the underlying message is always, "Subordinate your needs to meet mine." Children become stuck at an early age and do not learn to take risks. To assert autonomy from the parent is to court disapproval. The basic rules of dysfunctional families are learned: "Don't ask, don't think, don't feel." Numbing of the emotions becomes a way of dealing with the pain of the family.

There are certain parenting styles and behaviors that contribute to a lack of self-worth in the child. These include being hypercritical of the child, using withdrawal of love as a punishment and excessive physical discipline. Emotional neglect, and sexual and physical abuse by the parent are generally associated with poor self-esteem. Domination techniques, such as anger, fear, blame and guilt, to keep children in line are often found in families that produce offspring with co-dependency and other addictive behaviors. Double-bind messages from the parents add additional negative beliefs about self-worth. The practice of punishing children, and then lavishing immediate attention and love on them while they are upset because the parent feels guilty, contributes to a later life pattern of "Let's fight so we can make up and I'll feel loved."

Devaluation Of Self — Moral Masochism

The concept of co-dependency has been known about in some sense since the 1920s in the mental health field. Bits and pieces of the syndrome have been described by different psychologists. The early roots are found in the writings of Sigmund Freud, Carl Jung, Karen Horney, Alfred Adler, Erich Fromm, Esther Meneker and Bruno Bettelheim. Just recently the word co-dependency has come out of the addiction field tying together research and the different theories to form the label.

Erich Fromm is a psychologist who believes that the deep fears associated with separation set up conditions of anxiety in a person. The fear of being separate and alone is so great that the individual goes to any length to avoid it. Feelings of helplessness and immobility become greatly exaggerated. The fear of separation arouses feelings of guilt and shame. The child learns that submissiveness is the way to reduce anxiety and guilt. The taking care of, rescuing and giving over to other people's needs becomes a necessity of life because it helps the child feel good on a short-term basis.

Doormat behavior is an anxiety reduction coping mechanism. Co-dependent people perceive that someone needs help and become worried and anxious. They have strong internal rules that say they *must* take care of others. If they go against these rules, they are in conflict with their own strong belief system, and anxiety begins to build to an unbearable point. Moving into action to help other persons helps reduce the anxiety that they experience. They temporarily feel better until they see the next person for whom they feel responsible, thus setting up the cycle over and over again. In this cycle, they can avoid looking at their own problems.

The child tries to seek wholeness and tries to achieve balance but is caught up in equating love with doing for others. Learning to deal with the fear of separation and abandonment is one of life's tasks. In the *Empty Fortress* Bruno Bettelheim relates three distinct periods where fears of abandonment must be overcome as a psychological Rite of Passage. The first stage is during childhood when there is a risk in becoming your own person different from that expected by the parents. The second stage is the first serious romance with the opposite sex where there can be a giving up of individuality to become the expected version of the other person. The third stage is in old age where an identity of your own must be developed to keep loneliness at bay as the grown children are busy with lives of their own.

The object loss psychological research has examined ways that people deal with important losses in their life. Loss in early life has profound significance on our integrity of the identity, our physical well-being, our ability to love and decisions on how to live. If children's basic need of learning trust in infancy and early childhood is not met, they feel a threat to the self. They feel unlovable and fear that they will be abandoned. If they cannot have the love of the rigid, rejecting or alcoholic parent, or if they feel the threat of being deprived of the loving, benevolent parent, the stage is set for further loss and impoverishment. Choices that the child could make are narrowed out of fear. At some point children make the decision to abandon themselves. The little child self is abandoned to take on that adult role of taking care of those people in the household who are incapable of meeting that little child's needs for security, love and trust.

In her book *Masochism And The Emerging Ego* psychoanalyst Esther Meneker uses the term moral masochism to describe a pattern of co-dependent behavior that is a function of insufficient separation from the parent. It is present in some degree in many people and is to be distinguished from sexual masochism of a pathological nature. Moral masochism is *not* an unconscious need for punishment but is an adaptive defense mechanism to overcome feelings of conflict and anxiety based on the young child's fears of abandonment. Modern-day feminist writers describe masochism as a dependency issue rather than a pathological need for punishment. It is inevitable in humans because of the long emotional and physical period of dependence of the child on the family. Sigmund Freud wrote that moral masochism was a general life attitude. Karen Horney believed this pattern was the way the child learns to avoid parental conflict. The child learns a pattern of submissiveness to appease the parent, thereby bringing out the mother's maternal instinct ensuring that the evolutionary species will continue.

Children learn to discount their own wants in favor of parental wishes as a defense against separation and loss of the parents' love. Conformity by becoming a good little girl or boy is reinforced by the parent because our society values obedience. Because of the parents' pleasure at their children's compliance and displeasure at resistance, youngsters feel conflict and anxiety when they try to assert their own way. This is more likely to be true if children have a sensitive nature. They develop a strong sense of duty and by living up to high standards, their anxiety level is kept at a comfortable level. However, if they try to assert their own independence and meet their own needs, then they perceive themselves as selfish and anxiety again comes into play. When things do not go as they want, they tend to blame themselves, believing that they did not do enough. Failure to live up to their learned expectations as a caretaker can lead to a cycle of self-blame and depression.

Children who are brought up to overinvest their will in meeting the needs of others can believe in themselves only if they are valued by others. External validation is the way they try to booster self-esteem. They alternately try to please others to improve their lovability status and reject those who do not accept them. These placating coping defenses of the individual who has experienced nonpersonhood become a shield against despondency.

Idealizing their parents is one way children appease the guilt feelings that accompany the anger, which is perceived as unacceptable. Children may develop a coping style of overidentification with the parents' viewpoint. This helps deal with the conflict created by the ambivalence of wishing to conform to get strokes from the parent and to assert their own independence. Children may rationalize that what they want doesn't really matter.

This type of thinking represents a sour grapes belief system of "What Mom wants me to do is what I really want for myself." The pattern of devaluing the self is set in motion as a way to try to regain the lost love. The truth of the imperfect parent is too painful to bear and is altered to a more acceptable version. Faced with insufficient love, the child can distort reality and learn to survive on the illusion of the parents' love. Or the child can withdraw emotionally from the parent and engage in acting-out behavior. In some cases of child abuse or neglect, the denial of reality and suppression of the hurtful memories are necessary for the child to survive. There is a splitting of the self into different parts to deal with the pain.

If children's early needs for love and security are not met, they may go through life asking one basic question, "Am I lovable?" As they grow up, they may unconsciously turn to new situations where patterns of dependency and submission in relationships are repeated. They seek to re-create them with a dominant partner as they are familiar and comfortable in a vague sense. The old patterns of defense against the parental figure are transferred to the new love, friend or boss. They may seek out relationships that will replay these same situations over and over again drawing those who match their low self-esteem. Friendships that are developed tend to be shallow and unproductive. The pattern persists when choosing a mate, and the Doormat Syndrome is off and running again being taught to new generations of children.

Getting Off The Merry-Go-Round Of Co-dependency

The process of release from co-dependency is a process of rediscovering your true identity. It is a release from that little wounded child of the past and a relearning of thoughts, attitudes and behavior patterns that foster self-worth. It is becoming real by reconnecting with your True Self.

When you take responsibility for what happens and tune in to your inner direction for guidance, you learn to manifest peace and harmony in your life. You can learn to tune into the lovingness and the wisdom that says, "If you know in your heart of hearts that it is right, do it. If not, don't." Developing this inner aspect of yourself is a way to bring harmony and balance into your life.

Finding Your Inner Wisdom

Developing that deep sense of knowing what is right for yourself is a process that spans your lifetime. You can access information directly by asking your Inner Wisdom or Higher Self to help you. Your Inner Wisdom draws from your intuition, current information, feelings and thoughts, and from the deep knowledge of what is best in regard to your unique spiritual growth. Meditation, prayer and focusing your mind on a concern are all ways of directing your Higher Self to assist you. With practice you can have a dialogue with your Inner Wisdom on any topic you desire. As you follow its guidance, you will find you make wiser decisions that give you more confidence in its role in your life.

The Higher Self is within, waiting to be tapped. Close your eyes and get into a relaxed position. Focus your vision on the area between your eyebrows, and take 10 deep breaths. Set your thoughts aside as you ask for access to your Inner Wisdom. Visualize yourself on a journey that will take you into those deep inner recesses of yourself. See yourself on a giant spiral going down, around, down and inward to reach the Higher Self. Transverse this spiral of your inner knowing with each step you take bringing you closer to that Inner Wisdom. Acknowledge that loving and giving part which provides all the information you need. Continue going deeper and deeper by using the breath until you have a sense of calm and harmony.

Acknowledge that Higher Self part in all that it has provided for you in helping guide your actions. Thank it for responding to your request for help; daily gratitude and acknowledgment help keep you accepting of this unique part of yourself. Ask your Higher Self to continue to give daily guidance through your hunches, intuitive thoughts and creative ideas as well as messages from your physical body. Ask if it will communicate with you through your dreams and images as well as directly by using a yes or no response when you ask questions. By being loving and responsive to your Inner Wisdom, you can work out a means of communication that is best for you. Then you will need to be a very careful listener to the messages that you will be given.

Going around and around perpetuating the same pattern of errors on a merry-go-round is a metaphor for the Doormat Syndrome. Metaphors are symbolic representations of the way we look at ourselves. Looking at your metaphors can help provide a lovely process to stop perpetually spinning around, making the same wrong choices again and again. Using metaphors can be a means of addressing the attraction to the excitement and challenge of trying to change other people. Part of the transformation process is to choose new metaphors to counteract your settling for crumbs of hope that things will be better and the belief that loving must hurt. To change your metaphors is to change your identity so that you no longer need to be locked into a self-consuming relationship in your dependence for security.

Learning to catch the "brass ring of self-worth and get off the wheel" is an exciting journey. The process through co-dependency is developing that inner sense of self and a dependence on your deep spiritual nature. The process is developing self-acceptance and love, and learning to value self equally as other people. Personal integrity is expressed by taking responsibility for your own behavior and letting others do the same. When these skills are learned, then mature relationships that are characterized by a mutual commitment to growth and fulfillment can happen.

Trade In And Trade Up Your Metaphors

What is the metaphor that you give to yourself regarding your significant relationship? Do you view yourself as vibrant and healthy or defeated and hopeless? How do you see yourself: someone limp as an old dishrag, tame as a pussycat, caught on a hook, stuck like a tar baby, in charge of life as you move from one adventure to another, or dumped on? Make a visual picture of the primary way you characterize yourself by shutting your eyes and letting a picture come to your mind. Write it here.

_____

How do you feel about your metaphor? Does your symbolic image of yourself please you? Fill in the blank. When I think about my vision of

myself, I feel _____. Note if you are having difficulty identifying your feeling. If so, this may be an indicator that you are shutting down your feelings and becoming psychologically numb as a coping mechanism to deal with an unhappy situation that you don't want to face. Feelings are emotions that are sad, bad, glad, mad and *scadd* (that's southern talk for scared). Concentrate now on identifying how you feel.

The second step is to determine how you feel about how you feel. This is a deeper level feeling and is related to how you feel about yourself. Your feeling about your feeling is the self-concept. You can get in touch with your basic self-concept on any issue by determining how you feel about it and then identifying the feeling about the feeling. When I think about my feeling

about my metaphor identified above, I feel _____

_____

Now shut your eyes again and allow the metaphor to shift. Visualize it and allow some movement in your picture. You are the writer, movie producer, director and actor all rolled up in one. This is your story and you can change it to suit yourself. Gradually let that negative metaphor evolve into a more positive version. Trade in your old metaphor for a better one.

I have viewed myself as a _____ since _____.

Now I'm learning to become a _____.

I choose to see myself as a _____.
Think of other people you admire and give them a metaphor.

Person	Metaphor

List three other ways you would like to see yourself.

_____

_____

_____

Choose a new metaphor of yourself that you can carry out.

_____

Honor this new improved version of yourself. Visualize yourself acting in accordance with your new metaphor. As you go through your daily actions, check with your metaphor and ask yourself, "Is this the way I should act with my new view of myself?" Repeat this exercise several times if necessary to get that new picture of yourself. Then live it!

⁂ TWO ⁂

Choose Your Crazy Coping Patterns Carefully

(You'll Be Using Them For A Long Time)

My Goals For You

I want to love you without clutching,
Appreciate you without judging.
Join you without invading.
Invite you without demanding,
Leave you without guilt,
Criticize you without blaming,
And help you without insulting.
If I can have the same from you,
Then we can truly meet each other.

Virginia Satir

Irrelevant

Super-Reasonable

How You Cope Determines What Happens To You

All coping is a process of trying to obtain self-worth and act in ways that are familiar. The event or what happens, how you perceive and respond to it and the coping are all separate things. Virginia Satir says, "The problem is not in the event. The problem is in the coping." An event happens. Assumptions about what happened are triggered, based on our past associations with similar events. Old familiar feelings come forth. Then the coping or the way to deal with the event occurs. How we cope is based on how we feel about ourselves and our self-worth.

Let's take a look at how the different coping styles increase or decrease conflict in dealing with other people. Satir describes four dysfunctional ways of communicating with another person: blaming, placating, distracting and being super-reasonable. These are learned ways of acting and responding when there is threat or conflict in a situation. These dysfunctional stances cause a distancing of the individuals as perception of what happened is distorted through their negative emotions that arise. Even negative chemical changes happen in the body when the unpleasantness of the confrontation brings about the need to protect one's own point of view. Compromise and problem solving are rarely accomplished. We all have elements of these four stances in our repertoire of responding but we may favor one or two of them during conflict or confrontation. We may switch back and forth between them in any one conversation but we typically choose one or two ways of dealing with the situation.

One ineffective coping style is the Distractor. When faced with a threatening situation, Distractors feel insignificant, irrelevant and invisible. They cannot stand confrontation and distract others away from the pain by drawing attention to themselves or changing the subject. They are out of step with what is going on by acting silly, making jokes and disclaimers, or changing the subject. They become hyperactive and move around a lot. Because the appeal to forget about the conflict can be tempting, Distractors often succeed in temporarily waylaying the antagonism. The last children born in families may become Distractors as they take on that role to keep the peace. The message behind the Distractor is, "I feel unlovable when people fight. Pay attention to me and my bad behavior and forget about the conflict." Doormats may have an element of this coping style in their behavior.

A second dysfunctional style is Super-Reasonable. This style of unproductive coping behavior is based on the message, "I can't deal with this issue so I'll act bored and above it all." Super-Reasonable people stay rigid, keeping themselves motionless while looking down their noses at the others. Remember the Avoidant Attached described in Chapter 1? These types play it cool by withdrawing and distancing themselves from the problem at hand. They may act like a computer staying reserved and cold without any show of emotion, at least on the surface. Inwardly, they feel vulnerable and overwhelmed, and incapable of facing the conflict. Because they cannot deal with the problem at hand, they practice the fine art of nonclosure to a T by withdrawing emotionally so that things can never be settled. They may intellectualize, use big words or monopolize the conversation. Withdrawal or running away is the extreme Super-Reasonable stance.

A third coping stance is the Blamer who is the controller at any price. Blamers have a high need to win and may do so through intimidation. Even when they are wrong, it is someone else's fault. The blaming stance is the "High Muckety Muck" or "Bigwig" stance. The Blamer tries to get the other person to do what is desired through faultfinding, name-calling, criticism and anger. The assumption behind blaming is, "I am right and you are wrong. Do it my way." In their own way, Blamers are usually trying to teach others but they do it through aversive control techniques. The message behind the Blamer is, "I am internally threatened and frightened so I use critical verbal messages to make you feel frightened and obey me. I feel like a nothing so I must treat you like a nothing." Blamers stand ramrod straight, frown and glare while pointing their finger at the other person.

Because Blamers need someone to go along with their critical remarks, they usually hook up with a Placator. Placators are people-pleasers. Most co-dependent people have a heavy dose of placating in their interactional style with an occasional turning to blaming. Placators are afraid of being abandoned and fear rejection; as a result they use excessive yes behavior by agreeing and apologizing to keep others from becoming upset. Placating is the typical submissive role. Women in our society generally have been the placators, although some men have adopted this coping style also.

Satir estimates that 99 percent of the world operates with women as Placators kneeling at the foot of the male with one hand over their heart to express their unworthiness and the other hand outstretched to ask for forgiveness. The placating attitude splits people into good and bad — "I am nothing; you are everything." Placators assume responsibility for what happened and always feel at fault. They ask nothing for themselves but give all to others. They have a message imposed on their consciousness of "Don't let your needs be known. It is wrong to be selfish." Withdrawal, helplessness and depression are the ultimate placating behaviors.

Doormats sometimes cycle back and forth between placating and blaming, although the anger and criticism may be expressed indirectly or even internally. Doormats sometimes beat others to the punch and blame themselves in an attempt to ward off outside criticism and punishment.

Placating

Blamer

When Blamers and Placators come together, they usually interact with the Placators on their knees in front of the Blamers.

Let's Hear It For Congruence

Congruence is the name Satir gives to functional communication. Congruence is acting in accordance with your internal honesty by stating how you feel at the moment. Good self-esteem and health are manifested when the individual interacts with congruence. All body messages are the same; the internal emotions match the facial expression, body position, voice tone and the verbal message. There is no need to be in perpetual motion to distract, blame and criticize, withdraw into aloofness or give in. Congruent individuals speak the truth as they see it at the moment; what they say fits with what they feel and think. In congruence people own their feelings inside and make choices based on those feelings. If they are angry, they can state so. If they feel uncomfortable with what is going on, they let this be known. If the internal feeling is happiness or confusion, they respond in kind. In the congruent state, individuals are able to say yes or no, and can say what fits for them at that moment. Trust in oneself and the other person is communicated with the freedom to be straight and comment on the situation.

Five Freedoms Of Empowerment

Virginia Satir's Growth Model lists five freedoms that empower people. These freedoms are based on learning to communicate effectively and present oneself in a congruent way. In her *Process of Becoming More Fully Human,* Satir's freedoms state . . .

- The freedom to see and hear what is here, instead of what should be, was or will be
- The freedom to say what you feel and think, instead of what you should
- The freedom to feel what you feel, instead of what you ought
- The freedom to ask for what you want, instead of always waiting for permission
- The freedom to take risks in your own behalf, instead of choosing to be only 'secure' and not rocking the boat

A basic respect for everyone including oneself underlies the position of congruence. This functional coping stance has a belief system that all people are valuable and competent. All can learn to make the best choices in their own behalf. All have the right to make mistakes and learn from them. All can stand on their own two feet taking their senses of sight, sound, touch, smell, taste and sensuality into account, and respecting the truth that

Congruent

their body tells them. All can grow in intimate relationships with others if they honor that basic respect that can occur between two people and practice effective communication from a position of empowerment. The message congruent behavior gives is, "I value you and care about your wishes and I equally care about me and my wishes. We are people of equal value and we can work this out."

Most of us grew up in dysfunctional families where there were problems of poor communication and an imbalance of power. You couldn't choose your parents and relatives but you can choose your friends, workplace and spouse. You can create new families and functional systems for yourself in all areas of your life if you develop the positive communication skills that draw functional people to you. In functional systems, people have the freedom to be who they really are. They care for each other and share intimacy. They recognize each other's needs and pull together to mutually strengthen the relationship.

We create our own panoramas according to the belief systems that we hold. People with distinctly negative viewpoints will create distinctly negative happenings to accompany their version of how the world is perceived. If you want to know what is going on in your unconscious mind, just look at what you experience daily. It will be done to you as you believe. If there is constant pandemonium in your everyday life, it is time to clean the house. You can clear away the rubble of other people's negative voices and rules inside your head, and concentrate on your Higher Self to give you guidance. You have within you the capacity to make positive changes in your own behalf.

Ladies And Gentlemen, Take Your Positions

To fully understand Satir's stances you will need to experience them. The memories of days gone past and the emotional reactions that accompanied them are sometimes stored in the subconscious mind and the muscle tissue of the body. Taking the dysfunctional stance and exaggerating it can help put you in touch with events that are deep in your subconscious mind and in motor memory. Holding the stance until your muscles ache can put you in touch with hidden memories. This exercise will allow you to get in touch on a physical level with the dysfunctional stances you may be unaware of.

Put yourself in the blame stance. Stand straight, glare and point your finger while getting in touch with the stupidity and injustice others have perpetuated. Let the anger rise up in you and give it to them saying the words they need to hear for their own good. Hold this position and exaggerate it. Notice the effect it has on your body and the tension that is created. Visualize the effect it has on the persons you have imagined. Does blaming bring about the desired change in their behavior? Does the anger diminish their self-esteem as well as yours? Is there a better way that you can take care of yourself? Who used this position to control you in your child-

hood? _____ Who uses it now? _____
Whom do you blame on a regular basis? Another blame stance is to criticize yourself. Point the finger of blame at yourself. Where did you learn this

stance? _____

Now go down on your knees to the placating position. Put one hand over your heart saying, "Poor me, I'm so unworthy," and extend the other hand out to the other person as if to ask his or her forgiveness, or to show your eternal gratitude. Cry, appease, whine, apologize and bootlick to keep the other person happy at all costs. Notice how strained and uncomfortable your body becomes with no air in your rib cage and a continued looking up straining your neck. Get in touch with the emotions of helplessness and depression. Close your eyes and visualize the person who used this position when you were small. From whom did you learn this syrupy manner of

coping? _____ Did the other person find happiness in

groveling? _____ Did the other lead a life of bitterness or constant martyrdom? Close your eyes and project yourself 20 years from now, still on your knees and still trying to make it up to that other person. As an old lady or man, look back over your life as a Placator. Imagine you are talking to your little grandchildren. What could you tell them on how to act differently? Play out a dialogue with yourself on how you could have made it better for yourself.

Now go to the Distractor position. Here you are always off center and in constant movement to protect yourself and others from the separation and loneliness of the situation. Hunch your shoulders and move about, fluttering your hands while making irrelevant comments and jokes. Add some symptoms of a headache, an anxiety attack or other physical illness. Use your symptoms to pull the attention away from the confrontation. Notice your shallow breathing. Make this scenario stronger and stronger until you get in touch with how invisible and scattered you feel.

Next determine at what times in your life you have used this position to relieve the pressure that you were feeling during an uncomfortable situation. Listen for the Distractor-type phrases you have made in the past: "Pay attention to me, I'm sick. Don't be so serious about this. Live it up. Let's not talk about this now. Did you hear the joke about the . . ." Remember how you changed the subject to bring about temporary relief, but prevented others from coming to a solution. See yourself becoming too giddy or even drunk to deal with the pain of the moment so that you sedate the situation with irrelevant behavior. Think back to when someone in your family used Distractor behavior when you were small and determine what effect this behavior had on your family. Where did you learn Distractor behavior?

Aloof is the key word for being Super-Reasonable. In this enactment, feel disdain for the other person and the situation. Stand straight and tall looking down your nose on everyone being above it all. Do not react to anything and respond as a computer would without emotion. Use long words and a dry, dead monotonous voice. Lecture and talk in long paragraphs as you show the others how bored you are with the subject. Distance yourself from the situation with your coldness and superiority. Totally withdraw and leave the confrontation. How does Super-Reasonable behavior sap your life juices

and make you less than human? _____

See the cost of energy that is involved in maintaining such a rigid position of denial and withdrawal. Feel the internal "blahs" and lack of compassion and frustration over never getting a solution to a problem. Again check to

see who you learned this stance from in your early years. _____

_____ Well, how do you feel now? Did you get in touch with some of your crazier ways of acting? By assuming these positions, your body will give you information about how you cope. Take off all these roles of acting. Now breathe deeply and shake out all tension that is left over from taking these roles.

Now practice being congruent. Deep breathe as you stand centered, balanced with your feet placed firmly on the floor. Put your shoulders back and lift up your head. See how this position allows for the expansion of air in your lungs giving you energy. Notice how you feel. Practice stating your

feelings. How do you feel? _____.

Say it out loud. Say it several times until you feel confident. Now imagine you are angry. Feel the anger and tension well up in your stomach. Allow your body and facial expressions to convey what you feel as you say, "When

you _____, I feel angry." Practice this several times as you notice how congruent your posture, body language, and internal and external messages are. Congruence is practicing honesty of emotion. Repeat the Rule of Congruence over three times. "When I say what I feel in the moment, I am congruent." Now practice the exercise again with feelings of sadness and happiness.

As you learn to recognize these stances in everyday conversation, you will better understand how communication is facilitated or breaks down. Conversation in its reciprocal nature is like a ball that is being tossed back and forth. Each person throws the conversational ball to the others and they respond by throwing it back. One or more people try to stop playing ball when these dysfunctional stances are used.

Satir estimates that in the general population the coping response of placating is used about 50 percent of the time. Blaming constitutes about 30 percent of the communication while Super-Reasonable behavior is practiced about 15 percent. Irrelevance is used about 4½ percent of the time. Congruent communication is used only in ½ percent of the interactions. Recognizing the stances allows you to stand back and say silently, "I know what you are doing." As you learn to remain congruent, you can readily see how others try to control and manipulate through the dysfunctional stances.

Tallying The Stances

To gain practice on recognizing the stances, use Table 2.1 to code how people talk to each other. You could code politicians on television (watch how they distract and blame their opponent), your office workers in a meeting or the relatives at a family gathering (better do these last two in secret). Choose both peaceful and confrontational situations to see how dysfunctional behavior increases when the stakes are high. Tally how many times you hear the different stances communicated. Also tally your reaction to what is being said. Tally both the verbal statements and the nonverbal movements that accompany them. The purpose of this exercise is to make you more aware of how others use dysfunctional communication to control the situation and how you react during times of threat.

Ways To Measure How You Shut Up, Put Up With Or Bury

Doormats generally have some self-imposed limitations they have learned that perpetuate their staying on their knees. Co-dependent people have a high degree of passive-aggressive behavior. They may listen and agree but then go ahead and act in their own self-defeating way. Inside a stubborn little boy or girl may be silently screaming, "Hell, no. You can't tell me what to do!" Passive aggressiveness may be expressed with a "Feel sorry for me but don't tell me what to do attitude." It may also come out as "Yes, but . . .," the automatic answer when someone else tells you of the absurdity of your situation and makes suggestions on how you might make things better for yourself.

Table 2.1. Doormat Tally

The Other Person's Responses	
Verbal	Blaming
Nonverbal	
Verbal	Placating
Nonverbal	
Verbal	Distractor
Nonverbal	
Verbal	Super-Reasonable
Nonverbal	
Verbal	Congruence
Nonverbal	
My Reaction	
Verbal	Blaming
Internal	
Verbal	Placating
Internal	
Verbal	Distractor
Internal	
Verbal	Super-Reasonable
Internal	
Verbal	Congruence
Internal	

Table 2.1. Continued

Blaming	Aversive control techniques of faultfinding, criticism, name-calling and anger
Message	"I am frightened so I use verbal messages to make you frightened. I feel like a nothing so I must treat you like I am a something so you will obey me. I can teach you through my anger."
Placating	Agreement to keep other person happy, apologizing, yes behavior
Message	"I am nothing; you are everything."
Distractor	Uses irrelevant statements, jokes, disclaimers; changes the subject; is hyperactive to take attention away from the problem
Message	"I'm unlovable and can't stand to see people fight so I'll act up. Pay attention to me and my bad behavior."
Super-Reasonable	Above-it-all behavior; withdrawal and distancing from the problem; nonclosure of the problem
Message	"I can't deal with this so I'll act bored. I'll act superintelligent and above it all so I won't have to face this."
Congruence	Internal feelings, body language and words are all equal: stating facts, staying in context, stating opinions, setting limits for others, assertive (not aggressive) listening at a deep level, using statements that signify self-esteem
Message	"I am a worthwhile person who can speak my truth at the moment; I choose to stay centered and not to get caught up in your dysfunctional communication."

Passive-aggressive behavior is another form of using denial as a coping mechanism to deal with pain. It is a distraction-type stance to excuse away the inappropriate and inconsiderate behavior of others, and overlook things that would make others stop and shout, "Hey, wait a minute here!" Doormats tend to deny themselves the very thing they need most — self expression. Doormats typically have learned to numb their emotions and not express their feelings by using denial as a way to cope with some of the pain. They develop an illusion of safety in specific areas so that they do not have to deal with reality.

Pride appears to be an underlying mechanism in some people's co-dependency. They may take secret pride in how strong they are and how much they can take. This "No matter what, I can take it" attitude is dangerous because it encourages others to heap it on. Doormats are great in addition and look for extra burdens to take on, but they rarely are good at subtracting the unnecessary weight from their shoulders. In the next section an exercise suggested by Virginia Satir graphically illustrates this point.

Feeling The Weight Of The World

How much are you willing to add to your own dose of daily stress in order to be of help to others? Let's find out. For this exercise you will need to enlist several other people to help you. They will represent how much unnecessary responsibility you are willing to take on your shoulders. They will be living symbols of how you allow others to dump on you, lean on you and give you their problems. In this exercise they symbolize unnecessary burdens that you carry on your shoulders.

If you have a bad back, have the other people stand behind you and find a pressure point on your upper back or shoulders. Have them push on the pressure point to represent the weight. If you have a strong back, have the others hang on your back in a dead weight position. Have the people say statements that represent your adding more responsibility. They might say, "I need your help with this," "I'm so weak and helpless," "Worry about me," "Help me, help me," "Do this for me," or "Bail me out, will you?" to represent the added burdens.

Observe your reaction to the added pressure and stress. Did the additional pain or weight make you more determined to keep on going no

matter what? _____.
Did you deny how difficult it became and turn it to body pain? _____
Did you acknowledge it and say, "Stop. That's enough. I can't help you

because I've already got too heavy a load"? _____

Did you tap into secret pride that whispers, "Give me more. I can take it"?

_____

How do you feel about your reaction to being dumped on? Does it make
you angry, sad or want to laugh? _____ Look
at your coping with this event. Write down your feelings and reaction.

_____

_____

How do you feel about the emotion you felt? _____

_____

How did your body register the pain and tension? _____

_____

In what other situations have you felt the same sensations that you experienced in your body during this exercise? _____

_____

Now close your eyes and determine the others that you typically carry on
your back. _____
Be aware of how carrying the weight of other persons is detrimental to you.

What effect does it have on you? _____

_____

Visualize how your carrying them prevents them from standing on their
own two feet and doing what they need to do for themselves. How does

your taking them on your shoulders cripple them? _____

_____

Feel once again how difficult it was for you to sustain all that extra weight
on your back. Know that you have choices on how you can do things
differently. Get in touch with what is best for them and for yourself. What do
you want to do with other persons who are hanging on to you for dear life?

_____

_____

That's right. Just let them go. Ask them to stand on their own two feet and take care of their own needs while you do the same for yourself. If you can't let them go, read more of the book and come back to redo this exercise. Feel the difference in your back and posture. Now, doesn't that feel much better? Breathe deeply and congratulate yourself for this great accomplishment of learning to subtract what you no longer need — dead weight on your shoulders.

Now, talk to your pride. Yes, you can have a dialogue with those different parts of you that have interfered with your personal growth. Tell your pride about your need to stop taking on the unnecessary weight of others. Ask it to find other places for it to attach to that will be of value to you.

Denial is a coping mechanism that has some value because it is necessary for us to believe that we are safe in the world. We cannot be worrying about every single thing all of the time because we wouldn't have any time left for just plain living. However, denial becomes counterproductive when we refuse to examine those painful areas in life that could be made better if we took in new information and made the resolution to change.

Crapola Index

Doormats have a low "Crapola Index." They allow things to happen to them that they would yell, "Faddle or bosh!" if someone else were asking them for advice on the very same thing. Overlooking harmful things to yourself is a form of denial that is based on being stuck in a large number of counterproductive rules about how things must be. The ideal position is to take a "no nonsense" attitude about how others treat you and correspondingly how you treat others. The Crapola Index is a measure of how much you are willing to pull the wool over your eyes and what you are willing to put up with on a daily basis.

Determining The Crapola Index

Give yourself a rating on your Crapola Index. On a scale of one to ten, with ten being the highest and one being the lowest, where do you place yourself in pulling the wool over your own eyes? If you put up with a lot of the "old you know what," then your level might be a nine. If you don't sell yourself a bill of goods most of the time, you might be a three or four. Be

really honest here. Determine your personal Crapola Index. _____

Now take the Crapola Test and list those things in your daily living that you "overlook," and pretend to others and yourself that they really don't matter. Somewhere on a different level you know they really do. Take out your "detector" and be truly honest with yourself. The purpose of this list is not to make you angry with other people but to bring those matters to your conscious awareness that you have been repressing. The Crapola Test is an honesty test — self-honesty. Ask your Inner Wisdom to assist you. State your issues here.

_____

_____

_____

_____

_____

There, how did you do? Did you uncover some things that are not acceptable to you that you have been putting up with just to keep the peace? Now give yourself a rating on the Crapola Index where you would like to be.

_____ For example, if the issues secretly bothering you that you typically overlook were previously at a nine level, where would

you feel comfortable? _____ What level do you

want in your honesty with yourself? _____

You can learn to take a no-nonsense attitude in life: Graphically speaking that is, "I don't dump on other people and I don't allow them to dump on me." You can learn techniques of communication that allow you to express yourself in ways that show you equally value your needs and those of others. The no-nonsense style also means learning ways to deal with manipulative and controlling behavior of others, and not doing any of these yourself. This style is a way of thinking and acting that is basically honest and respectful both of yourself and others. By coming from a position of mutual respect, you can feel more comfortable and honest in your daily interactions.

How gullible are you? Were you one of the last children in your class to stop believing in Santa Claus? Doormat people, being of a sensitive nature and believing that they are not worthy, sometimes allow themselves to be patronized. They settle for the crumbs or the crust of the bread. They accept the lesser half because they are not worthy enough to take a whole piece or a piece with lots of frosting. They are easily appeased and seduced by a "There, there, there," and a pat on the head. They allow the shuffle of gaining immediate attention and sympathy instead of holding out for a settlement of the real issue. They are satisfied with words and empty promises, such as "I'll change" or "We will work it out," when there is no accompanying plan of action.

Hope springs eternal in the breast of co-dependents because they want to believe the best. This is another form of denial for co-dependent people. They deny the belief that situations will remain the same. "Things will get better" is the secret hope. This attitude allows them to continue in relationships, marriages and jobs for years. The wanting to believe is so entrenched that they overlook personal inconveniences again and again until they turn into major annoyances. It takes an incredible amount to harden their common sense to a point where they are willing to take a stand. Gradually or abruptly the realization dawns that they are no longer willing to overlook unacceptable behavior. They may blow up but it can turn into a fizzle with the other person calming the waters and saying, "There, there, things will be different," when in fact they will not. Or they blow up with a self-rationalizing anger that provides the energy to make something different happen.

The Chicken Index

All of life is ceaseless change. The only thing that never changes is change itself. Of all human aspirations, security is the least admirable and the hardest to achieve in this world of constant change. One indication of personal maturity is your ability to handle change or even to promote it to further yourself. The Chicken Index (initiated by Chicken Little himself) is your ability to take risks in your own behalf to make things better for yourself. It is the ability to look at new beliefs, information or situations, and decide what would best fit you. It is related to facing your fear, and then going ahead to make something new and exciting happen. It is also a measure of your need to prevent change, and your resistance to shaking up circumstances and challenging the status quo.

Determining The Chicken Index

Let's determine how you view yourself in the area of risk taking. A score of ten means you take high risks; a score of one means you vegetate and refute change. Think back over the decisions you have made over the past few years. Has change been thrust on you or have you gone out and shaken your own tree to get new fruit? Does the thought of something new and out of the ordinary strike fear in your heart, causing you to run and cry, "The sky is falling! The sky is falling!" Or does change make you tingle with excitement as you bring forth your problem-solving skills? Determine your

Chicken Index. _____

If you can't give yourself one overall number rating, break down the risk-taking areas in your life and give yourself several indexes (your primary relationship, your parents, your career, etc.). Don't feel bad if your ratings are low. Risk taking is a skill that can be learned with practice in a safe

setting. Now, where would you like your ratings to be? _____
The discrepancy between where you are and where you would like to be makes an impact on your self-esteem. List the areas of your life where you have taken risks and they have turned out well for you.

_____

_____

_____

_____

Now activate the part of your brain labeled "Looking out for my best interests." Look around for some activities that you have been thinking about and really wanting to do but were afraid to do. Make a list of these.

_____

_____

_____

_____

Tuck these activities away, and take them out to look at now and then. Someday when you are feeling adventuresome, you may want to try some of them. How about a new metaphor for yourself? Here is a good one: "The woman or man who goes from one challenge to the next!" Try it on and see if it fits some part of your daring nature that has previously been in hiding.

Squelcho Index

Another rating you can give yourself is the Squelcho Index, which gives a yardstick of how much you are willing to shut up. Edith Bunker inspired this rating; she had a very high rating in this area. All Archie had to do was say, "Edith, squelch it!" and she automatically shut up in midsentence. People with high Squelcho ratings come from families where self-expression is not allowed. When not being squelched by someone else, Doormats keep their own thumbs tightly on their own head to hold themselves down. Or they may gripe and complain to others but rarely address the issue directly with the person that they need to settle up with. They believe that others prohibit them from speaking out but in actuality it is their own feeling of insecurity that prevents them from saying what they feel and think. Griping to oneself only results in permanent lip lock. Pushing down one's feelings and desires on a regular basis causes anger to build up to a degree where it has to explode. Long-term Squelcho behavior typically leads to the feeling of not being appreciated and the "poor me" attitude of martyrdom.

The real issue is learning to feel comfortable about speaking out. One rule taught in Alcoholics Anonymous groups is, "We are as sick as we are secret." Doormats grew up in families where some people were allowed to state their opinion but others were not. The message may have been, "Children should be seen but not heard." Children may have internalized a rule that says, "I'd better be quiet so I won't get ridiculed or hurt." Fearing rejection, they have learned to keep a lid on everything for self-protection. Their message to themselves while growing up may have been, "To be loved, I'd better keep quiet. I'll clam up so I can be accepted." And while this may have been true for the little child, this is a false assumption for an adult. Adults can make decisions that they couldn't as a child to speak up and protect themselves, and leave situations that are threatening to them.

The psychological research shows that assertive people are more respected than those who let others walk all over them. Respect is earned by speaking out for what you consider to be fair. Communication is improved when you can ask for information about yourself and others, and clarify assumptions. The research also shows that assertive people who make things happen for themselves feel better about who they are.

Determining The Squelcho Index

Now here is your chance. Make a list of all those things that you have squelched or had stuck in your craw these many long-suffering years. Write down the issues in your life you would like to discuss with someone but in the past have felt afraid to.

_____

_____

_____

_____

_____

Think of an issue in your current life where you feel you have not allowed yourself to express your own opinion. List that issue here. _____

_____

What would happen if you spoke your mind? _____

_____

What is the absolute worst thing that would happen to you or the other person? _____

_____

Would you feel afraid and uncomfortable? _____ Would you just die? _____
Would there be physical violence? _____ Would the other person get their feelings hurt? _____ Write the very worst thing that could happen here.

_____

_____

Now check your assumption. Is this likely to happen? What is another alternative that could happen? _____

_____

What is a positive alternative that might come about? _____

_____

Close your eyes and visualize the worst happening. Allow the worst to simply happen in your mind. Notice the bodily discomfort you have as you play through the scene to its completion. Did you survive the worst? Carry the scene forward and see how you can move through the conflict to a more positive outcome. Carry it on into the future while feeling good about your ability to effect positive change.

Learning to speak out is a process you can practice and learn. First, give yourself permission to state your opinion or wishes in a certain area. Gather your thoughts together and visualize your making positive changes on your own behalf. In the situation, speak gently but firmly. Stand up straight on your own two feet and state what you want. Breathe deeply if you feel anxious. Respond to the other person's remarks with dignity. Check inward to see how you feel about speaking out. While you are learning, it is more important that you feel better about your assertive act than its outcome. Know that you can ask for what you want but don't become addicted to getting it.

If you are concerned about your ratings and your lists are lengthy, you might consider taking some courses in effective communication and assertive training so that you can learn ways to be more honest in your interactions with others.

As you progress in your recovery from co-dependency, you will become more congruent. Learning to be congruent is to seek wholeness both for yourself and those with whom you come in contact. Freedom is a state of liberation both from the control of another person, and from the self-limiting belief systems and ways of coping. The opposite of freedom is dependency, be it on an addictive substance or an unhealthy relationship with another person. Kahlil Gibran said, "What is freedom but the fragments of yourself you would discard to become free?" The greatest freedom is to be free from a life of self-doubt and eternal conflict. As you grow both psychologically and spiritually, and gain deep inner guidance, your choices become more wholesome and congruent. This is living at the level of the heart.

Mental Housecleaning

Just as we occasionally must clean house on a deep level to get to hidden dirt and to reorganize our belongings, it's a good idea to tidy up our personal life. Look at your life situation. Using the list of Doormat characteristics listed in Chapter 1, determine what areas of your daily existence do not work well for you because you have given away your power.

Shut your eyes and center inward. Breathe deeply and let your mind wander to a belief about yourself that you would like to change. As you continue to breathe deeply, let your unconscious mind make a picture of your body and the areas that are dusty, dirty and disorganized. Step back and view yourself as a professional housecleaner might, getting an overview of those areas that could stand a good scrubbing.

Using this visual image to represent your life, choose a figure of someone to go within to do deep cleaning. It could be a fictional character such as Mr. Clean, a symbol such as a tornado, someone you know such as your persnickety Aunt Jane or even a miniature version of yourself. Visualize this person gathering the necessary equipment together to make a clean sweep of the cluttered image of yourself. See your housecleaner of choice move into your body to start the task. It's a dirty job, but somebody has to do it!

See what areas are in need of change. Notice the disrepair, clutter, dirt and grime that need a good shaking. Gather your tools — brushes, brooms, vacuum cleaner, cleaning sprays and powders — and get down to it. Clean each area using whatever it takes to get the spot bright and shiny. Throw out any garbage you find. Mentally sweep everything from your head to toe, removing all that is not necessary. Look for any unproductive thoughts and stuff them in a heavy-duty garbage sack. Look for belief systems about yourself that are self-defeating. Find behaviors that do you in every time and remove them. Vacuum all corners and crevices taking up any gray or black areas. Keep the garbage sack and the vacuum cleaner bag tightly closed, and take them out to the trash bin. See the garbageman come and carry it away to the dump where it is covered with dirt and buried. Continue to clean and polish all areas of your body — your mind, brain, heart and any other areas until all are squeaky clean.

Now stand back and survey your effort. If there are any empty spaces, let them be filled with positive thoughts. Feel the satisfaction of work well done and the benefits of your effort. Don't you feel fresh and revitalized? Breathe deeply as you pat yourself on the back.

❧ THREE ❧

Who's Really
In Charge Here?

---

*Once the game is over, the king and the pawn go back in the
same box.*

Italian Proverb

Do As I Say — Power, Its Form And Function

There is an ancient South American legend that tells of the time when the
gods created the earth. They looked for a place to hide power because they
recognized it was a possibly dangerous force that might be found and used
in a destructive fashion. They considered the top of the mountain and the
bottom of the sea but ruled these out because power was too dangerous to
hide in one place. They decided to divide it up and place it in the hearts of
men, women and children.

All human beings have a drive for power; it is the essence of survival.
Power drives start in infancy and continue throughout life. The word power
is derived from the Latin word "potre," which means "to be able." The
sense of being in control is crucial to well-being and positive mental

45

health. Power drives enable us to exert control over ourselves and our environment in order to survive. While individuals may differ in their need to be in control, feeling competent and being in charge of one's environment are universal needs.

Power is the ability of the individual to produce an intended effect on another individual. It is morally neutral and can be used to gain good as well as bad. There are two basic categories of power. Coercion is gaining compliance through physical force or verbal threat. Persuasion is the power of authority that is based on an acceptance by the person because of past conditioning to social norms.

Some types of control are adaptive in that they strengthen self-worth. Having an internal sense of control results in individuals taking responsibility for what happens to them. Current research supports that increased personal control about simple everyday life choices affects achievement and job success as well as overall mental health. Other power needs result in maladaptive social control based on manipulation drives that result from anxiety, fear and threat to self-esteem. This type of control can become an addiction.

Power relationships start in childhood when children learn to give in, distract, ignore or use anger with their parents. Learning a power base starts in infancy when children learn to command their parents by crying or by being endearing. Children learn ways to cope with the inequalities of power (smaller size, younger age, lack of financial clout) by being cute, by asserting their independence or by giving in to the parents' wishes. Parental attitudes and the type of discipline used determine acceptable and unacceptable ways of acting in the family. Self-esteem is innately tied to how children feel about the ways they express their personal power.

The gods, in placing the power in the hearts of men and women, did not take into account the different ways it could be twisted and misused. The model of power that has been operating in our world for thousands of years is one of domination. Ego power has been defined as the ability to control others to get one's own needs met. In different cultures and ages, the age-old theme of misuse of power has been played through again and again: One person or group of people claim superiority over another person or group and use adversive means to subdue them.

The first law of power is "Them that has it tries to keep it." Remember the childhood game of King or Queen of the Hill? The object was to use brute force to remain in charge. As youngsters we were taught that power was dualistic because it is based on either "If I have the power, then you don't," or "If you have the power, then I won't have any." Power could not be shared. It had to be protected lest the other person wrestle it away. This type of mind-set creates power struggles, anger, tension and competition.

The old domination/submission model has been a great waster of human potential for both the dominant person or group as well as the submissive person or group. It has fostered destructive behavior, aggression and violence on the part of those in control. It has encouraged resentment, contempt, passive-aggressive behavior and rebelliousness because it was necessary for the submissive person to learn manipulation to survive. This old model stifled the growth of both victim and victimizer as it precluded trust, affection and true intimacy.

Is Your System Open Or Closed?

Family systems theory shows how the actions of each person in the family affect the actions of others. A system is a group of people who come together and interact on a regular basis. Your family, office and church group are all systems. Family systems theory discusses how relationships can be opened or closed. All relationships are energy exchanges among the members of that system. The type of coping styles and the maturity level of the parents define the degree to which a family's system is open or closed. If the marriage is unhappy and dysfunctional, the children will display characteristics of this also.

In a closed system, energy is spent in trying to keep things from changing. One or more members in the relationship may invest in keeping everything at a status quo. The power structure is in a continual state of imbalance. The dysfunctional coping stances help preserve the closed system as ineffective communication prevents problem solving and forward movement. Rules within the closed system function to keep a lid on everything with an unspoken agreement that things must remain as they are. The roles of the different people in the system become rigid. Individuals who are dependent on alcohol or drugs as well as those with power or sexual needs invest much time and effort in preserving the status quo. As long as things remain the same and they continue their unproductive behavior, there is no motivation for them to change. Individuals who grow up in closed systems do not get their early emotional and psychological needs met, and develop the compulsive behavior that is typical of addictions

In an open system, energy is spent in promoting change, and there is a balance of power. Keeping everything fixed and stable is not as important as the growth and development of all of the individuals. The open system provides increased energy that transforms the whole system into something new. In the open system, individuals are treated with love, respect and concern, and the family members are allowed and encouraged to function productively and grow.

Systems sometimes change with time. When one partner grows and the other does not, there is bound to be conflict. Take the case of the woman who is ready to be open and has chosen a man whose needs are to be shut down (or vice versa). Their personal needs for communication and congruence differ greatly. The conflict may intensify as they try to convince the other one of the rightness of their own position. With the number of opportunities for promoting self-growth increasing through workshops, television and self-help books, as well as the feminist movement that encourages self-expression, it is no wonder that relationships are changing drastically.

The Power Lineup

Visualize how the people in your family would line up if you had to designate their order from the most powerful to least powerful. Who makes the decisions in your family? Who has the right to tell whom what to do? What is the pecking order or the chain of command? Make a power lineup or use an organizational chart to show how the individuals fall. You can do this exercise both with your current family and the family in which you were raised. Write their names in order of where they fall. Draw your lineup here.

How did you do with this exercise? Was it easy for you to decide who went where? Is your lineup polarized from most to least? _____ Is it balanced such as a circle or triangle? _____ Is it top heavy with too many chiefs and not enough braves or vice versa? _____ Does age play a big part in your family's decision about who holds the power? _____ Is the right to make decisions for others static or does it shift according to the situation? _____ What topics are rigid and unnegotiable? _____

_____

Who made the rules behind the decisions on how power should be

distributed? _____

Is the power malevolent or benevolent? _____

Is it direct, manipulative or subtle? _____

What methods of control are used to keep people in line? _____

_____

Who has the reputation of needing more control than others? _____

_____

Who has the reputation of needing more help than others? _____

_____

Which individuals have to give up their personal power and how do they

react? _____

_____

How do you feel about where you fall within the lineup? _____
What is the price you and other family members pay to maintain the balance

of power as defined in your family? _____

_____

The Continuum Of Power

A continuum of power shows how unchecked power needs of either the submissive or dominant person can turn into dysfunctional ways of living (see Table 3.1).

Alfred Adler, an early theorist in the field of psychology, said that unresolved ego power needs in a person come from a sense of inferiority. The psychological research shows that individuals who have strong needs for ego power and domination over others are also weak in their ability to love and feel affiliation for others. They need to maintain control more than

Table 3.1. Continuum of Power

Co-dependency	Mastery-Oriented Behavior	Dependency/Dominance
Being controlled by others; trying to control others by passive-aggressive behavior	In control of oneself	Control over others; being controlled by addictions
Very little power or power through manipulating others	Equality of power	Too much power or power given away to addictions
Too much value given to others	Equally valuing self and others	Too much value placed on self
Taking care of the needs of others	Taking responsibility for self and allowing others to take care of themselves	Having others take care of oneself or alienation from others

they need affection and intimacy from others, and use any means necessary to remain in charge. This is the second law of ego power: "Them that has it sometimes have to resort to foul means to keep it." Dominant individuals have the ability to persuade others to go along with them. They also have the facility to persuade themselves that what they are doing is correct. They rationalize their attack or withdrawal regarding an issue because they believe they are acting in the best interests of others. They view others as weak and not capable of making decisions on their own behalf. The third law of ego power is: "Them that has it feel justified in whatever means they must use to keep it." Self-delusion is part of their coping style that is necessary to rationalize their actions. Sometimes people may seek out controlling mates to reproduce a well-known pattern from childhood with which they are familiar. They may need someone who can make decisions for them so they can remain in the helpless role and avoid responsibility. Satir describes two patterns of being a dictator and controlling someone else: the malevolent type who controls with coercion and oppression and the benevolent type who controls through loving kindness. The outcome is the same: to keep other people under the thumb and not allow them to grow up and make choices for themselves. Benevolent dictators are very seductive to most people. They charm and win others to do things their way through positive expectations and reinforcement.

Benevolent dictators want to be the Dear Abby of the universe and offer solutions to everyone else's problems except their own. They may even be correct in their assessment of how things are and know how to correct them. However, with their high degree of emotional involvement, they are often caught up in a power struggle without realizing it. They become enmeshed in an obsessive need to change the other person. They rationalize their need for control by saying, "I just want what's best for him. If only he would live up to his own potential." Knowing what is best for other people can be a subtle form of blaming. It elevates the knower to a higher position while deflating the others by defining what is wrong with them.

Benevolent dictators can become so caught up in other people's problems that they unconsciously use others to avoid the personal responsibility of looking at their own actions. They can play the role of the expert who gives advice as a coping mechanism to avoid looking at their own unresolved needs for power. They elevate themselves to the role of the expert and treat other people as problems, taking the attitude, "What is the problem today that I can help you with?" rather than, "You are a valuable person and you have the resources to make your own decisions."

Doormats generally have learned to give their power away or use it in a passive-aggressive fashion that is manipulative. Powerlessness can be used as a way to get power in a paradoxical way; sometimes the most powerful person in the household is the one who withholds what others want as a means of feeling in control. The housewife who can't get organized enough to clean the house and the older child who wets his pants are examples of passive-aggressive behavior that focuses on controlling the only aspect of the environment that is within their control. Attention and being relieved of responsibility are the payoffs that are often given for passive-aggressive behavior.

The need to control other people's behavior is a tendency that was learned in childhood. Doormats are the opposite of those who dominate and although they have high needs to feel secure and attached to others, they still have the need for control. They have strong needs to constantly seek approval and affirmation. At some point in their early childhood, they have made an unconscious decision to take care of others as a way of feeling important and powerful. If they do not feel that their self-sacrifice is appreciated and acknowledged, they tend to become bitter and view themselves as victims.

People who are co-dependent often use techniques of the benevolent dictator to control and manipulate others. Placators often hold power in the family through their passive-aggressive behavior and their martyr status. They have high expectations for other people. They have a list of "shoulds" for someone else as well as for themselves: He should stop drinking; she should stop running around and get better grades; well, if he/she/they

would just _____

(fill in your own blank here).

Affirmations To Set You Free

Affirmations are positive thoughts that you choose to put in your mind on a regular basis to counteract a negative pattern of thinking. Affirmations can be practiced daily so that they become immersed in your unconscious mind to bring about the desired change. At some level of understanding, you may be aware that you are powerless over other people's use of alcohol, drugs, sexual addiction, excessive workaholism or unacceptable behavior, but you may still be preoccupied with trying to force change. If so, you have yet to learn that you are responsible only for Number One — yourself! You can use affirmations to help erase old negative thought patterns. Set up a schedule of affirmations that you can review many times a day. Make a list of the following and post them on your mirror, car and kitchen sink, and by your bed. Say to yourself at least several times a day:

- I choose to think in a positive manner about _____.
- I can only change myself. I allow _____
  to take care of themselves.
- I am responsible for my own actions and thoughts.
- I allow _____ to take care of
  their own lives.
- I am me and I let _____ be who
  they are.
- I am a worthwhile person capable of loving and being loved.
- I am calm and loving about this positive action.
- I am a competent, powerful person.

Doormats seek a replay of the childhood scene of taking care of the sick parent. You may have even been attracted to others because you felt that they needed your help. You may have so gradually been drawn into the caretaker role that you assumed responsibility for them even in areas where they could have taken care of themselves. When there is this high degree of enmeshment, there may be feelings of guilt if you cannot prevent or control what others do. You may even have progressed to a point where you allow yourself to be ridiculed, blamed or physically abused because you believe that somehow it is all your fault. This is very destructive behavior on your part and it comes from your unconscious, crazymaking set of rules that you carry with you at all times.

Giving advice and telling others what they should do is always dangerous because it is simplistic and does not take into account the underlying reasons for the dysfunctional behavior. There is an underlying element of "You must do as I say because I take care of you, give you money, bail you out or spend a lot of time on your problems." No matter how the advice is couched, there is a conditional expectation for change. There is a sense of "owing" because of the personal investment of time and effort that builds in a resistance to change on the part of other people.

Generally people know what they should do to make things better for themselves. They know they should eat more veggies and exercise more. They know they should stop smoking or drinking, be more organized or leave an abusive situation. Advice giving lets people down because they may not have the personal resources to carry through on what has been suggested and may feel an even heavier load of guilt for not being able to act in a mature manner. There is disappointment for advice givers when the others do not carry out the suggestions.

To change your co-dependent behavior, you have to change your expectation for the situation or other person. Expectations are like traps; you can get caught in the thinking pattern of "Things must be this way for me to be happy." This one-sided way of thinking will surely make you miserable as things rarely turn out the way you expect. For the sake of better mental health give up the "shoulds" for others and learn how to change your unrealistic expectations.

If You Don't Like The Picture, Tune In A New Channel

Here is a visualization exercise that will help you view other people in a different light. Quiet your mind and body while you count backward from ten to one. Allow your thoughts to be still while you seek your Inner Wisdom. Enlist its help in adopting a new perspective on the person you are concerned about. Breathe deeply and be aware of the powerlessness of your attempts to change, manipulate or control. See how your efforts bring about no result except to further mire you in a no-win situation. Be aware of the excessive amount of energy you have expended at your own expense. Acknowledge how your overinvolvement and worry have prevented you from looking at your own problems.

How do you feel about your past behavior of taking care of you from other people's needs? _____

Is this feeling comfortable for you? _____ How do you feel about your

feelings? _____

Would you like to change your feelings? _____ What do you want to do

about them? _____

What is your longing regarding your need to be overly involved? _____

Know, really know, that you are learning new ways of thinking about respecting other people and yourself. Be gentle with yourself as you realize that you have had a lifetime of thinking and acting one way. Now you are learning new ways of being. Give yourself permission to release other people from your personal responsibility. Tell yourself, "I need not be their teacher." Repeat this phrase to yourself over and over until you believe its truth. "I need not be their teacher. My need is not to judge. My need is to be me." This subtle message has such power in it. It does not mean that you give up influence. You model how to live in the highest way possible. As you expand, you allow room for other people to respond in kind.

Give yourself permission to take all the time you need to learn this new and challenging skill. Breathe deeply and relax more and more as you focus on respect — respecting yourself and respecting other people. Repeat to yourself, "I respect your right to be you and I respect my right to be me." Thank your Higher Self for taking this opportunity to allow some new perceptions about the situation.

People do not heal when there is control and demand in the guise of love. Instead of viewing people with problems as riddles that you must solve, a more enlightened approach is to see them as the opportunity to learn a skill or lesson. Sometimes the only thing you can do is listen to the story. You need not feel that you must come up with a solution. When you are at a place where you don't need to solve anything but only listen, then you know you are making progress in refraining from Doormat behavior. Another helpful strategy is to listen for the underlying concerns and give other people information and alternatives rather than solutions. This approach releases the need to control and manipulate, and focuses on what they need to learn rather than what is wrong with them.

Dealing With Crumb Bums And Other Congenital Grumps

One of the challenges in life is to learn to deal with people who use adversive control techniques to try to keep you in line. Adversive control includes using demeaning, confrontational behaviors such as glaring, sighing, blaming, and yelling "#, &, % and @!" These are negative power techniques that may have worked for people in the past so they continue to use them. The need to avoid confrontation is monumental, tapping directly into the fear of the Doormat. You may have learned to cope with negative energy by engaging in placating behaviors.

In *The Fire From Within,* Carlos Castaneda calls people who use adversive control "petty tyrants." A petty tyrant is someone who bullies, torments or otherwise oppresses you. Examples of strong men standing up to petty tyrants include Christ before Pilate, Sir Thomas More before King Henry VIII and Mr. Roberts before the ship's captain in the movie, *Mr. Roberts.* In each case, the hero stood firm, calm and collected in the face of persecution. Castaneda says that to stumble onto a petty tyrant is lucky because you can learn about control, discipline and self-respect in your dealings with him. There is a challenge to dealing with impossible people in positions of power. He even recommends that you go out and look for one so that you can practice facing them with discipline and inner strength.

Strong techniques are needed to stand up to petty tyrants. Certainly, to join their own game of anger and recrimination is useless because they can always muster up more negative energy than you can. Pleading, placating behavior is music to their ears. Reason and rational suggestions may not be enough for them to give up their adversive power. Stronger techniques are needed!

One way to deal with situations of blame, criticism and ridicule is to show you are not intimidated by their tactics. Stand firm and focus on your own truth. Stay centered in what you want and do not get carried away by blaming. Draw yourself up, push your shoulders back and stand directly on your own two feet. Expand your own power base by deep breathing to quell any anxiety you may feel. Focus on a spot between their eyes while you deal with your physical reaction. Define who you are and what you stand for. State where your personal boundaries are and what you will and will not allow:

- I understand you are angry and I will not allow you to call me names.
- I won't stand here and let you yell at me.
- I don't want you calling me loving names in a sarcastic tone of voice.
- I won't talk with you until you can speak in a normal tone of voice.
- I want you to stick to the topic of the conversation and not get sidetracked in blaming.
- I choose not to get in a power struggle with you about this. Let's back off for a while.

By the same token, you do not give away your power by blaming the other person. As you stand firm and focus on what you want to have happen, the situation can be defused. With this attitude, "I respect you; I respect me;

we can work this out but only in a manner that is good for both of us," there is more of a likelihood of a reasonable outcome. Mutual respect and offering a solution while allowing the other person to save face is the powerful message that was behind Gandhi's position of nonviolence that presented a new model of dealing with unfairness and aggression.

Remember, people have no power over you save what you grant them. No idea, belief system or group can sway you unless you agree. You always have choices and need not remain in any situation where you are mistreated. You can choose to hold on to your power. You also choose to give it away. You write your circumstances by your own thinking and how you allow others to treat you. Tell others of your strength and both you and they will come to believe in it. Speak your truth daily by stating what you want in a loving manner. Learn to add the loving "and . . ." statement that states what is consistent with your integrity while expressing concern for others:

- I must stand firm on this for my own self-respect and I'm seeking a way that preserves your own self-regard.
- I choose not to . . . and it in no way diminishes my love for you.
- I feel strongly about this and I care deeply about you.
- This is not for me and I thank you for sharing it with me.
- I must do this and I am worried about the effect it might have on you.
- I love you and I love me too. We can talk about this and figure it out.

Doormats often become unglued when they are criticized. They have thin skin that allows nasty words and labels to penetrate, and go directly into the heart like little barbs. They may buy into the critical remarks that erode their self-respect. They have never learned the technique of filtering out the information that is given in the criticism from the negative comments and put downs. When you were a child, angry words may have had the effect of making you feel even more small and helpless. Now as an adult, you can choose to act in a different way instead of giving up your power to feelings of helplessness and guilt. You can emerge as a master even in threatening situations where you would have previously felt overpowered by negative words.

Handling criticism, both just and unjust, is a high level skill that can be learned. Anger is an energy of a negative force. That is all that it is.

When you realize that anger is simply negative energy that is used to try to change your behavior, you can put it in a proper perspective. Here is a technique that uses the principle of *akido* to deflect negative energy back to the perpetrator and prevent your becoming emotionally involved with the negative insults that are being heaped on you. The purpose of this technique is to desensitize you from your overactive fears about being yelled at and criticized.

Putting Up Your Shield

To prepare mentally for brow-beating and name-calling, visualize yourself putting up a shield for self-protection. Choose the type of shield that fits you best. Your armor may be made of heavy metal or clear acrylic, or it may be made of a gossamer fabric. Choose the material that will provide the best protection from acid remarks. The shield will allow helpful information to get through. The shield protects you only from blame, unjust criticism, and remarks like "@, & and %." You don't want to block out feedback that will be helpful to you.

Use the imaginative powers of your mind to place the shield in front of you, and feel how safe and secure you are. Nothing can penetrate the shield unless you allow it to come through. Notice how your skin is becoming thicker, acting as a second shield so that you choose what is allowed into your consciousness. Now visualize a petty tyrant calling you names and trying to unnerve you. View the words that come out of the tyrant's mouth as negative energy in written form like you see in cartoons. Criticism is just misguided energy. See how it moves through the air toward you as a negative force about which you can make choices. Visualize it as arrows, spears or slashes from a sword.

The negative energy signals you to put up your shield. You are safe from the verbal insults of others as long as you choose to be. See the slurs and slings fall off your shield, keeping you free from the negative energy. See how the angry remarks fall to the ground, go around you, over your head or bounce back to the speakers. Imagine them disarmed, being caught in a barrage of their own doing. Envision yourself standing straight and tall, proud of your accomplishment of deflecting unnecessary criticism. Remember that anger is sometimes used to instruct as an attempt to change your behavior. Being the wise person that you are, decide to look behind the anger to see if there is a message for you. Allow any information that is needed to penetrate your shield. This is a very clever shield; it can discriminate between what is good for you to hear and what needs to be discarded.

First, practice different versions of confrontations with different difficult people over and over in your mind. For the second part of this exercise you will need a partner who will yell at you so that you can practice putting up your shield automatically when you hear angry words. Have the other person get really mean, rough and nasty while you stand cool and collected. If you cannot rustle up a willing partner, then find a tape recorder and record all the nasty things that have been said to you in your entire life. Again visualize your sloughing off the unnecessary hurtful remarks.

Balancing The Seesaw Of Power

The gods were correct in their choice of putting power in the hearts of men, women and children. They did not realize how long it would take for humans to learn to use power correctly. It is almost as if the world had to misuse power over the centuries to come to a place where individuals can use it for empowerment of all. Now as the world is evolving in thought and consciousness, newer models of equality and mutuality regarding the use of power are being developed. Gandhi and Dr. Martin Luther King have demonstrated how to use methods of peace and nonviolence to bring change. Techniques of conflict resolution based on mutual respect and a win-win philosophy are changing the course of world history.

Current spiritual practices show that development of one's own personal power on a nonego basis is a satisfying, strengthening position. As you deepen your spiritual nature, you will view power in a more constructive and loving way. The proper use of power is viewed as the ability to do or act as an energy or force that produces results rather than having control or authority over others. Ego power reflects separation and control: "I am above you. I know what is right for you. You must do as I say." True personal power is gentle and free from the negative emotions of fear and distrust, and the accompanying manipulations. It is knowing who you are, stating your own truth as you see it and allowing others to do the same. Knowing your personal power is to be deeply in touch with your compassion and to know your strength in your vulnerability. Personal power when shared expands so that there is enough for all.

As individuals learn to grow in their own personal power, they give up the need to control others either through domination or manipulation. The stances of blaming and placating are not necessary when responsibility for one's own actions is the goal rather than trying to change the other person. The mature individual who experiences personal power does not need to deny others the opportunity to make their own decisions and learn from the consequences. Individuals can come together as equals to share information and examine alternatives.

Empowerment through love can become the purpose of interpersonal interactions rather than having power over others or being under their control. Personal power can be learned by staying in touch daily with the three Rs: Respect for self, Respect for others and Respect for property. Personal power also draws from the power of love, which is the strongest force in the world. Become aware of your personal power by acknowledging it daily. Once you learn to take your personal power, you have to learn to keep it.

Knowing Your Own Personal Power

Stand and bring your personal power to one place by closing your eyes and breathing deeply. Plant your feet firmly on the ground and feel your connection with the earth. Visualize deep, deep roots going from your feet into the earth to give stability. As you stand with this wide base of potency, focus on the strength that is within. Breathe deeply, knowing you are in touch with the power of the universe. Allow personal, loving power to circle through you, flowing in the top of your head, passing through your body and going into the earth where it recycles to the universe. Visualize yourself impervious to being knocked over by using this position of strength. As you stand on your own two feet with your shoulders back and your head held high, you can look at "what is" as reality. You can state your truth from a position of vitality and force. Now go deeper in your knowing to that inner circle of personal power that is based on your vulnerability and respect for the dignity of yourself and others. See how you share your power by your loving actions, and how it then increases empowering both of you. State the following affirmations as you pull the power of the universe through you by deep breathing. State the following words out loud in your Power Voice. Practice saying them in a loud voice until you really believe what you are saying:

- I am a woman/man of power.
- I center myself drawing on that internal strength from within.
- I stand tall and proud of my ability to draw from my own strength.
- I acknowledge the deep resources of my Inner Wisdom from which I draw.
- I empower myself and others through my loving actions.
- I celebrate my ability to love myself and others.
- I am a woman/man of true personal power.

❧ FOUR ❧

Survival Rules –
Past And Present

---

*You have learned what you have learned very well. It has helped
you survive.*

Virginia Satir

Those Old Family Rules

Several decades ago psychoanalyst Karen Horney described the "Tyranny
of the Shoulds." The shoulds are those internal statements we make that keep
our lives in constant check. Virginia Satir calls the ways that we limit ourselves
"Old Survival Rules." Survival rules are negative beliefs and behaviors learned
in childhood that helped the child cope and survive in the family. They are
often covert and are taught by nonverbal messages as well as spoken
language. Subtly taught to control children, they say, "You have to, you ought
to" or "You must." They are the commands (do, don't, can, can't) and the
polar values (good/bad/wrong/right) with which we were raised.

At one point, the family rules were necessary to help little children avoid
punishment, rejection and abandonment. The rules helped protect children

at a time when they had little personal power. They are based in fear and literally keep children alive because their origin is derived from threats and pressure of those in authority. The freedom to comment and say what you see, hear, think and feel is limited in troubled families. Children who are not allowed to express themselves grow up using a lot of childhood energy by becoming rebellious, passive aggressive, placating, super-reasonable or irrelevant.

Healthy families have rules, of course. Yet functional families provide a framework of guidelines rather than stringent rules. Guidelines are organizing principles that serve to give general information without the contagion of the negative emotions. As an adult, you can examine old family rules to see if they help you cope productively with life's problems or if they dominate your life in a negative way. Survival rules differ from one's true values, which reflect self-respect and integrity. A test of whether a rule fits your grown-up adult self is whether it allows you to continue to grow and develop a new sense of maturity.

Survival rules begin with an "I must always . . .," "I should always . . .," or "I could never . . . ." Because of a lack of self-sufficiency, life is lived with continual "Thou Shalts" and "Thou Shalt Nots." The survival rules are absolutes allowing for no deviation. They keep the person tied up inside because they are unrealistic and irrational coming out of the negative emotions of fear, guilt and shame. They may have worked for that little child but they no longer work in a grown-up world. Yet the person is tied to that little child mentality because by following these rules, conflict and anxiety are kept to a minimum. To transgress the rule is to go against a lifetime of tradition.

Behind almost any continual conflictual area of a person's life is a whole host of survival rules. Satir says, "We grow up being taught to be good, be quiet, don't rock the boat, and for God's sake, don't let anyone know what you're feeling! We have followed that recipe for being good and in the process have lost ourselves. . . . We need guidelines, not rules." Some of the survival rules that Satir has seen in families are:

- "I should be judgmental and angry if someone doesn't meet my expectations.
- I should give the nice face while stabbing myself inside.
- I should not make any mistakes while others are screwing up royally.
- I should always be completely fair in this world of unfairness.
- I should be grateful even though it is shit and they call it 'cold cream.' "

Co-dependent people seem to have an excess of survival rules. That's part of the pattern — taking on an abundance of negative characteristics from the troubled family. The "should list" of the Doormat centers around themes of striving for perfectionism, reacting to authority, appearing strong, denying feelings and self-expression, and keeping a lid on topics that are not allowed to be discussed. A running list of a Doormat might include being perfect, being submissive, not allowing feelings and being strong.

Being Perfect

- I should always look good.
- I should make everything in my life perfect or I am a failure.
- I should always be liked by everyone.
- I should never make a mistake.
- I should always be rational and fair while others are allowed to lose their heads.
- I should always say the correct thing.
- I should try harder to be perfect, then things will be better.

Being Submissive

- I should never rock the boat.
- I should never speak up and express my opinion.
- I should never argue with those in authority.
- I should make others feel good at my expense.
- I should take care of all situations where someone else feels bad.
- I must always make the peace and not allow people to argue or fight.
- I should always take the least part.
- I should give everything and put my needs aside.

Not Allowing Feelings

- I should never get angry.
- I should deal in thoughts and not emotions.
- I should never talk about how unhappy I am.
- I should deny my feelings when others express strong emotions and deprecate me.

Being Strong

- I should always be strong.
- I should never be ill.
- I should never ask for help.
- I should do it all by myself.
- I should always be healthy and energetic.
- I must continue taking care of others until I am depleted.
- I must rescue those who are in trouble.

- I must work harder and take over the responsibilities of others.
- I must continue my workaholic lifestyle to avoid looking at the real issues in my life.

Do you have a rule that says one thing and another rule that is exactly the opposite? This is called a double bind — two opposing messages are given about the same thing. Double-bind messages really cause crazymaking behavior because you try to keep them both and there is no way to win. The classic double-bind message is the nursery rhyme in which the daughter asks to go swimming and the mother says, "Yes, my darling daughter, you can go to swim, but don't go near the water!" A double-bind message might say, "I should be quiet around authority, and I should ask those in charge for things that other people want." Another example would be "I should never make a mistake while I see others around me making mistakes." The result is inner conflict because when you try to carry out one of the messages, the other surfaces with guilt and anxiety.

Discovering Your Old Survival Rules

Close your eyes and listen to the voices of your childhood instructing you on how to act. Think of the conflictual areas in your life where you feel limited by a vague sense of discomfort. There is probably an old rule for you here. Start out by thinking, "I should never . . .," and "I should always. . . ." Write down all of your survival rules.

_____

_____

_____

_____

_____

_____

_____

Look at the general themes of your rules. Group them according to category. Your categories might include those mentioned before, such as submissiveness, strength, perfectionism, etc., or they might be grouped around issues of alcohol and drugs, sex, success or failure, money, religion or relationships. Some rules may fit into two different categories.

Names of categories. _____

_____

_____

_____

_____

_____

What are the general childhood squelch messages behind your rules? List your rules in these specific groups.

Don't Comment	Don't Feel	Don't Touch	Don't Trust
_____	_____	_____	_____
_____	_____	_____	_____
_____	_____	_____	_____
_____	_____	_____	_____

Determine which rules are no longer in your best interests. Write down the out-of-date rules that no longer fit you.

_____

_____

_____

_____

_____

Holding It All Together

Doormats keep busy trying to hold all these rules together. In a stressful situation, Doormats feel uncomfortable as an old rule surfaces. They have to act on that rule to keep the anxiety level from going higher. When negative emotions are refuted and action is taken to help someone else, then the status quo is restored as the person acts in accordance with that which is familiar — the old family rule. Temporary comfort is bought but at the cost of self-esteem. The feelings that have been denied behind the rule may register as tension in a chosen part of the body such as a headache, a stiff neck or an uneasiness of the mind. Often back and neck pain develop as Doormats typically carry the weight of the world of other people's problems on their backs. Depression or a physical illness may develop in the attempt to live up to unrealistic self-expectations. Survival rules are innately tied to suffering because they represent psychological mechanisms that distance us from the sense of selfhood.

Day-to-day internal messages and interactions with others define us anew each day. Each limiting survival rule is connected to a valuable lesson with which we are being presented. The conflict experienced when we are in a situation that triggers the confining rule actually represents an opportunity for growth. What has been learned can be unlearned. Contrary to popular belief, old survival rules are not written in stone. There is a formula that you can rework over and over until the rule is changed into a guideline that is comfortable for you. By transforming your rule into a guideline, you will gain freedom of expression. Rules are absolutes; they do not allow for exceptions. Guidelines are a way of looking at a specific situation and gaining possibilities, alternatives and choices. Guidelines allow for flexibility according to the appropriateness of the situation that you face. Your choice is either to continue as is in the confusion of poor self-worth or to search for new ways of thinking and acting that can set you free.

Transforming Old Survival Rules Into Guidelines

You are now ready to make a change in your life by shifting one of your old survival rules. Because it has served you for so long, you will not be asked to get rid of it. But you can change it to make it fit your present interests. You won't be asked to throw it out completely. The old original rule will always be there if you want to bring it out, dust it off and use it should the rare occasion arise.

Write a rule that limits you or drives you crazy by running your life:

The "shoulds" are often equated with the "wrongs" of life as defined by someone else. Whose voice are you carrying around in your head? Maybe it is not your own "should" at all but someone else's. Maybe this dictate that you have been blindly living by is just a critical voice from your past that you have associated with a negative body state when you don't carry it out. When you stop and think about it, maybe all that is wrong is your internal feeling of discomfort surrounding this issue. Whose rule is this anyway?

Now ask yourself why. "Why should I follow this rule blindly?" _____

_____

Any time you hear yourself say, "I should . . .," tell yourself, "Aw, come on!

Why should I?" What is the worst thing that would happen? _____

_____

Why shouldn't you follow this rule? _____

_____

Look to see if there are other rules that apply to the same area. Rules learned in families tend to cluster around themes. Write down other rules that are connected to your first rule.

_____

_____

_____

_____

_____

Look at the humor of your always trying to live up to your rule. Visualize yourself going through the day obsessively and rigidly following that "should" rule. If you have chosen a "should not" rule, make a mental picture of how you would look in chains, ropes or gagged so that you could not follow the rule. Visualize yourself worn out and frustrated in trying to follow the unrealistic dictates of your rule.

How could you change the "should" so that it would be easier for you? Remember all of life is choice and you have learned to think this way so you can unlearn it. Rewrite your old family rule as a "could." Take the absolute out of your rule. Make it specific to a certain situation and allow yourself the choice of when and where you will follow it. Say to yourself, "If I really wanted to I could . . ., but I choose to . . . ." Now rewrite your rule in many different ways. For example, "I should never disagree with those in charge," could be changed to, "Sometimes I can choose to disagree with those in charge," or "I can redefine what 'in charge' means so that I can choose to speak out more." This exercise helps you learn to give yourself more choices!

Continue playing with your rule, stretching it out. "I choose to speak out in this certain area because I have some knowledge." "I realize that in this situation, it is appropriate to speak out." "I can feel good about speaking out about. . . ." "I can say what I want without getting nervous." "I can speak out when I have something important to say." "I can disagree just for the heck of it!" Go as far as you can with this process while noticing how you feel as you play around with the rule. Go for the ultimate breaking of the rule. "I can speak out whenever I want to!" There, did the heavens open up and strike you dead?

Remember, if you change your language, you can change your life. As you change your rule in this step-by-step fashion, monitor your inner comfort level to see if the changes fit with your Inner Wisdom. Now go through the process of transforming your original rule.

Step 1

Step 2

Step 3

Step 4

Step 5

Continue changing the rule until your formerly rigid rule becomes a guideline that you can comfortably live with. On another sheet of paper you can go through this process with other survival rules.

Now for the test! Go out and find a situation that will enable you to practice your new version of your rule. Go into easy situations at first as you get used to these new ways to act. Later you can try out tougher situations. As you practice your new learnings watch how you feel inside. It's all right if you feel scared; that just means that you are experiencing something that is new for you. Honor the fear and allow it to transform into excitement. Reward yourself for risk taking and trying something new. You are a risk taker. At this point, it is more important that you feel good about challenging the old rule than getting what you want out of the encounter.

❦ FIVE ❧

Doormat Talk

Never mind what others do; do what is right in Cosmic Truth
for you . . . . Begin by seeing that something in you
needs correction. That is your perfect start.

Vernon Howard

You Determine Your Worth

Not wanting others to think badly of us is a natural human emotion. Positive regard of others is a valid way of affirming ourselves as being worthwhile. Friendly words and gestures are ways of validating the essential goodness of our nature. It allows us to look at a corner of ourselves, to buffer the negativity of others and deal with self-doubt. In a larger sense, admiration and compliments allow us to deal with the issue of separation and possible loss. There is a fear of being rejected by those we care about or those in power. Rejection implies a threat to one's personal domain or a loss of reputation. In times of insecurity, we might feel threatened by the possibility of loss of attention, time, friendship or support of those we care about.

Overdependence on other people's ideas and opinions is the hallmark of the flaming co-dependent. You may have been scolded in the past as a child and told, "What would people think if they could see you like this? What would the neighbors say?" Embarrassment and shame became associated with misbehavior. The negative feelings associated with being judged by others and found wanting, rise to a peak during the teen years. This is when peer pressure becomes a way of life in an attempt to gain social acceptance. Remnants of this guilt and anxiety carry over into adulthood and continue to run your life.

The overwhelming need to seek the positive regard of others is based on some faulty assumptions: There is a single way to act that is accepted by all people: Perfection of thoughts as well as behavior is to be desired. You should be a superman or woman no matter the personal cost. • Your worth is determined by what you do or say rather than who you are. • Feeling good is determined by forces that are beyond your control rather than your internal nature.

These irrational beliefs set the stage for continual no-win situations. Dependency sets in when personal energy is consumed that could be spent on problem solving and creative projects.

Those who are driven to excess by love and caring have a different language than other people. If you are a hard-core student of co-dependency, then you are doomed to perpetual atonement for past, present and future sins. Your language will reflect your need to depend on that external reference for validation. Doormats turn their personal power over to someone else in the ways that they communicate. For example, the statements, "Whatever you want is okay," and "It's all right with me," may creep into the Doormat's conversation. Communication with others will have a subtle, self-deprecating "I'm no good" message. "You are so smart/great/right while I am so dumb/insignificant/wrong," is a typical theme. Doormats ask for permission to do things that others take for granted, and go ahead and do without asking. They request things from others more often than stating what they want. There is often an excess of apologizing for any discomfort that comes up in a situation as co-dependent persons assume that they are continually at fault. Those who deal with Doormats recognize the submissiveness behind such statements and begin to take control of the situation. They consciously or unconsciously realize that they are being offered everything on a silver platter and take advantage of Doormats. It's as if Doormats wear a T-shirt saying, "Available for demeaning!"

Beliefs are built on past experience. Up to a moment in time our belief systems about ourselves are all we know. Our core beliefs form our reality. Daily practice of a limiting belief entrenches it in a negative game that is played. The limiting beliefs link together into broad areas about life to form an overall self-concept. Some examples of erosion of self-worth are evident in a co-dependent person who says, "I can't keep a checkbook — I'm just no good with figures," or "I wish I could say no to my lover — it's easier to go along with what he wants." Listen for the dependent "should" messages behind your statements in relationships that do not work for you.

Belief Statements For A State Of Continual Imbalance In A Relationship

- I don't deserve. . . . It doesn't matter that much anyway.
- To feel loved and accepted, I'd better keep quiet about this.
- I don't care what happens to me as long as . . . is taken care of.
- I'll bail you out. Let me handle it.
- It's okay for me to give in as long as the relationship is preserved.

Belief Statements For A Balanced State Of Being In A Relationship

- I can ask for what I want knowing that I won't always get it.
- My self-worth depends on my asking and not my getting what I ask for.
- I feel happy when we share equally. We take turns getting our needs met.
- I choose to compromise rather than give in to keep the peace.

Sometimes Doormats are afraid to speak out because they believe they will hurt other people's feelings. This fear, which can be a powerful deterrent to speaking out, is merely learned behavior. It is learned in households where adults have used becoming hurt as a technique of discipline for the young child. It is a control technique of "If you don't do what I say, I'll be hurt and be disappointed in you." Children who are overly sensitive to the moods of adults and feel responsible for keeping them happy, greatly fear being abandoned by their parents. To survive they learn to keep quiet and overextend responsibility for others. They feel guilty when they transgress their internal rule of not speaking out. Keeping quiet is a way of protecting themselves from guilt and anxiety.

Believing you are responsible for someone else's feelings is grandiose thinking. You are not so powerful that you can influence how another person thinks and feels. The belief that you influence others' emotions comes from your need to control the situation and feel safe. You can only state your needs and how you see things. Other people can choose to feel hurt or not, based on their level of maturity. Their feelings are their responsibility. Watch your intention. If your intention is to speak the truth as you see it, then their choices are up to them. Your pussyfooting around is a hidden message to them that they are weak and can't take the truth. It is also your fear of conflict. By not speaking out, you are dishonest with yourself and others. If you agree to be silent and take on the brunt of the situation, you prevent growth from happening for each of you.

Right Speech

Right Speech means being as honest as you can be with yourself and others. Sometimes the best thing you can do is speak your truth and clear the air. As you learn to speak your feelings and ask for what you want, you will find that many of your fears about hurting others have been exaggerated. Some of the time the other people won't be upset and may be grateful that you have brought the needed topic out in the open. They may have a similar rule about not hurting feelings so nothing ever gets resolved. Intimacy can develop only when honesty and trust are present.

Co-dependent people are "outers." They depend more on what others think of them than on their own opinion of themselves. People who have self-reliance and rarely seek outside validation are "inners." There may be many areas where you give credence to other people's opinion rather than listen to your own inner knowing. People who live a tightly controlled, rigid life will have more areas where they are trying to please someone else other than themselves. Individuals who have learned to live spontaneously have learned to shelve some of their worn-out childhood scripts of "What will people think? What will the neighbors say?"

The key to understanding your issues in this area is to keep in mind the concept of excessiveness. Doormats are overly concerned, caught up in and just plain obsessive about the opinions of others. Other people can shrug off outside criticism or take it in stride. Doormats who have sensitive natures do not handle criticism well and overreact either by trying to become all things to all people or becoming angry.

Releasing That Childhood Script Of "What Will People Say?"

Here is a checklist to determine how much of yourself you hand over to other people for their opinions. Check all that apply to you and reevaluate whether you want to live in this self-afflicted nuttiness that keeps you caught in co-dependent behavior:

_____ My security stems from what others say about me.
_____ My fear of rejection determines how I act in a situation.
_____ I value others' opinions of how I do things rather than my own.
_____ I delay feeling good about what I have accomplished until someone else tells me I have done a good job.

_____ I put my true values aside to meet the needs of others in a situation.

_____ My self-esteem is lessened if someone else does not recognize my efforts.

_____ When someone criticizes me, I feel devastated.

Some of the areas in which Doormats turn over their sense of well-being to other people's opinion follow. Which areas are you the most sensitive about? In what areas have you become hardened by telling others to shove their critical remarks? Check your tender spots of concern.

Physical Appearance	Personal Characteristics
Face	Intelligence
Body	Communication skills
Clothes	Psychological coping skills
	Physical Fitness
	Morals

Skills And Talents	Possessions
Managerial skills	House
Mechanical skills	Car
Cooking skills	Wealth
Housekeeping skills	

Select an area where you choose to feel bad because of what someone else says about you. Write it here. _____

Close your eyes and go inside to consider if you are ready to shed some new light on this issue. Breathe deeply and get in touch with your Inner Wisdom. Talk to your inner guidance about how this concern has kept you from being free for many years. Tell it of the hurt and disappointment that you have felt trying to be what others have wanted of you instead of who you truly are. Have a dialogue with your Inner Wisdom; talk about your needs at this moment in time as you are learning to draw from your inner resources instead of gaining validation from outside sources. Ask your Higher Self to give you what you need to gain permission to change your beliefs in this area of concern.

Breathe deeply and repeat this formula to yourself: "I release myself from outside opinion on _____. I choose to follow my own guidelines instead of others'. My opinion of myself is what counts. I choose to give myself valid feedback and not seek validation from others. I choose to feel good about all that I do."

Validate what you have learned by examining your emotional state and the tensions in your body. How do you feel about what you have done? Determine your resolve to make this change in your life.

Right Speech is a way of speaking and organizing thought that comes from the Buddhist tradition. Right Speech means abstaining from telling lies; backbiting; slander and judgmental statements; harsh, rude and abusive language; and idle, useless chatter. This includes statements that you make about yourself as well as others. Right Speech means treating everyone with respect including (and most important for the Doormat) yourself. It can be a therapeutic technique that can be practiced as a kindness to yourself and a way to increase self-esteem. Using Right Speech is a means of being clear, courteous and ethical with yourself and others. Right Speech means listening to your language and making a conscious choice about how best to present you to yourself and to the world. Treating that which is holy with respect is the major principle of Right Speech.

Language defines us. It helps us find a voice for all that is beautiful within us. It can also do the opposite by being critical and petty. If what we think is what we become, then surely what we say is truly what we are. Using language carefully means not speaking carelessly or at the wrong time or place. When you abstain from negative speech you naturally gravitate to speaking positively. In the Buddhist tradition, if something useful cannot be said, the "noble silence" is kept.

In addition to these ancient spiritual practices, psychology and modern day spirituality are giving other ideas on how to use language to define ourselves in positive ways. Listen to yourself and to what you say and think as different events happen during the day. Consciously monitor your verbal and nonverbal reactions to get a better understanding of how you view the world and yourself. Take data on your thought and speech patterns. Be aware of the discomfort in your body when you say certain things and act in certain ways that are not consistent with who you really are. Our bodies provide marvelous feedback in terms of feelings of embarrassment, anxiety and even physical symptoms when what we say or do does not fit.

Stamp Out The Negative!

Most Doormats have a secret list of negative adjectives that they call themselves. They call forth these put-downs and insults when they are angry with themselves and feel the need for punishment. Write down your list of

negative, self-demeaning phrases. _____

_____

_____

_____

Categorize these adjectives according to the broad areas such as physical characteristics (fatso, skinny), mental competence (dumb, stupid, slow), or psychological traits (lazy, hot-tempered):

Physical Characteristics   **Mental Competence**   **Psychological Traits**

_____   _____   _____

_____   _____   _____

_____   _____   _____

Choose a label you would like to stop using. Ask yourself the following questions:

- Who has called me this in the past? _____

- What situation brought this label about? _____

- Is this adjective an accurate assessment of me? _____

- Is it okay for me to be this way once in awhile? _____

- Is it helpful or harmful for me to call myself this? _____

- Do I want to change how I feel about myself in this area? _____

- What kinder thing could I say to myself in this circumstance? _____

Give yourself permission to change this negative thinking pattern. Visualize the behavior or mistake that triggers the negative label and see yourself acting in a new way. Write the label down on a small piece of paper. Stamp on it. Jump up and down on the paper until it is demolished. Stamp out that negative. Whenever you slip and call yourself the negative label, smile and thank yourself for the reminder that you don't have to do this anymore. Or you can stamp your foot in reminder.

Cleaning up your life by cleaning up your language is a basic rule that is taught by most contemporary spiritual teachers who work to change negative belief systems. Energy follows thought. You actually become what you think. Say and think only what you want to become true in your life. If you don't want something to happen, don't give it energy by thinking about it. Use words that promote acceptance and tolerance instead of those that promote separation from your True Self and from others. Learn never to say things that limit you or another person. For example, say, "I made an error when I . . .," rather than, "I am bad, stupid, etc." State undesirable characteristics about yourself as temporary conditions or lessons to be learned rather than absolute facts. The "I am . . . and that's it" type of statements can be modified to include a time frame, taking into account that you are learning something new or the lack of effort that you are willing to put into something to change it. In this framework, "I am fat," could be changed to, "I'm temporarily fat." "I'm no good in math," could be changed to, "I'm just not willing to spend the time and effort to become proficient in math." When nagging, critical self-statements creep into your thoughts, change them by making an immediate positive affirmation.

Listen to your language for words that limit you rather than affirm and empower you. Words like "can't, never could, trying to, hope or plan to" all suggest the possibility of failure. Don't let your language limit you in any way. Positive statements about yourself will be more powerful when put in a forthright fashion in the present tense. "I am going to accomplish . . .," is a much stronger statement than, "I plan or hope to accomplish. . . ."

A *Course In Miracles* tells us, "Teach only love, for that is what you are." Right Speech urges us to think and say only loving things about ourselves and others, and to make corrections in a gentle and loving way when we slip up. Affirm daily to listen to your inner language as well as the words that you express orally. By listening with the heart and making good choices about all types of expression, you can promote harmony in your life and in the lives of those around you.

The Language Of Personal Power

Learning to ask for what you want is one of the greatest successes a Doormat can achieve. If you ask for something, you stand a 1,000 percent greater chance of getting it than if you don't ask. Being accustomed to taking the lesser part, it is often hard for co-dependent people to feel that they deserve good things to happen to them. The right to receive is a core issue with Doormats. Getting and taking are considered dirty words, while giving and helping are acts that are familiar. Doormats come from a generational tradition of giving, giving, giving and then getting mad because no one gives back to them. They then feel justified in becoming martyrs. Yet when they are the recipient, they feel strangely guilty. They have never learned the proper balance of giving and receiving that replenishes personal resources. They have never learned the social skill of allowing someone to gift them.

In the simplest sense, interactions are an exchange of energy accompanied by emotions and feelings about the acceptance between two people. A rule of thumb might be to get a return rate of energy to match the amount you put out. Asking for what you want but not being addicted to getting it is a sign of personal maturity. "I-messages" are an assertive yet gentle way to get your needs met without trampling on the needs of others. I-messages are statements of self-perception that focus on your important feelings and wishes. They are statements of your own needs and wants at the moment with the understanding that the other person also has needs and wants. I-messages express some of the vulnerability of the person by taking a risk in asking while using the feeling words: sad, bad, glad, mad and scad (scared). Examples of I-messages include, "I feel hurt inside when you call me names; instead I want you to tell me what you want changed; I want you to talk to me; I'm feeling lonesome right now; I wish you would express your emotions; I would like to know more about how you feel."

I-messages are effective because they do not threaten the other person's self-esteem. They give a clear statement about what is desired and lead to a conclusion rather than just hitting and running. They offer a choice of a solution to the problem being discussed and leave the topic open for further discussion. They require active listening to understand the other person's emotional reaction.

"You-messages" focus on the listeners and try to control their behavior. They often turn into direct verbal accusations or attacks on the other person. Responsibility for change is placed on the other person. There is an expectation for the other person's behavior that is not being met. They are the "shoulds" that are projected on someone else. Examples of you-messages include, "You should act nicer to my mother. You are being silly about this. You should pay attention to me."

Honor Your Needs By Using I-Messages

I-messages have three parts. They describe the behavior that is objectionable in a nonblaming way, express the primary feelings and state what the effects are on the speaker. Combining them with asking for what you want is a powerful means of communication. This course of action allows you to take responsibility for your own feelings and wants in a gentle, yet confrontive way. The goal of I-messages is to deal with problem behavior while inviting the other person to become more sensitive in order to produce change.

Practice changing some of these blaming statements into the I-message format.

Situation: Every day you are late for work because one person in the car pool is never ready to be picked up at the agreed time. The you-message might sound like this, "You make us all late for work. You are so inconsiderate." Change this to an I-message and ask for what you want.

Describe The Behavior	**State The Feeling**
When you are not ready,	I feel upset . . .

State The Effects On You	**State What You Want**
knowing I'll be late and start the day out rushed.	What I want from you is to be ready so that we can all feel good in the morning.

Situation: Your spouse or friend calls you names.

Describe The Behavior	**State The Feeling**
When you call me that,	I feel like a lost child . . .

State The Effects On You	**State What You Want**
and want to run away.	I want you to tell me if you are angry but stop calling me names. I would like to make a bargain to disagree without name-calling.

Now using the following situations, write in the I-messages. Your spouse is late in coming home from work. _____

_____

Your friend does not give you an answer and refuses to talk about something that is important to you. _____

_____

Your mother constantly interrupts you to state her opinion. _____

_____

Your daughter answers your request with a smart remark. _____

_____

Now write your own situation in here. _____

_____

Write in your I-message and ask for what you want. _____

_____

Do the same with another worrisome situation in your life. _____

_____

Write the new improved I-message. _____

_____

Remember, you won't always get what you ask for. There is no guarantee the other person will go along with your wishes. But you can feel good that you are speaking up, communicating feelings and stating your preferences in a clear way. Don't attach concern to the outcome but celebrate learning new ways of communicating.

You can go for a lobotomy of your soap opera mentality that keeps you enmeshed in conflict and crisis. You can learn to set boundaries for yourself so that others do not trespass on what you hold sacred. You can learn to speak from your heart instead of your guilt and state your truth in a loving way so that it does not hurt others. Moving through co-dependency means using the language of personal power to check out assumptions before reacting to them. It means learning to stand up to anger and criticism, and having the courage to stick to a controversial topic to work it through to closure. It means taking personal risks and shaking up those self-limiting belief systems. But it is possible. Stand up and ask for what you want. And if you don't get it, then acknowledge that you want it but your can't have it (at least in the fashion that you asked for it). Then regroup to determine a plan of acceptance or action and get on with it.

Now if days or weeks of practicing appropriate communication do not bring changes in the other person's behavior, what do you do? You have many choices. You can continue hoping for a change even though you suspect that the other person is interested in keeping things the way they are. You can get angry and blow up. You can give up and try to live with the unpleasantness. You can get angry and turn it inward to depression. You can continue complaining to your friends. Or you can state what actions you must take if the situation continues as is. This is called "upping the ante." You simply state what consequences you are willing to have take place if a change in the situation does not occur. It involves an "or else" type of statement made loud and clear. If the techniques of I-messages are not strong enough to get the other person's attention, then you may have to do something radical. Telling your boss politely that you must seek another job if your salary is not brought in line with others in the office, is an example of a risk-taking statement. It will bring results although they may not be the ones you desire. And you do have to be willing to live with the aftermath of your statement. After all, your boss, spouse or friend has heavily invested in keeping things as they are.

This technique does not mean making idle threats. Threats lose their effectiveness over a period of time if they are not carried out. This is a calculated risk on your part to determine a plan of action that you will follow through on and feel good about. Upping the ante is sometimes an action taken out of frustration when you come to the realization, "I'm mad as hell and I'm not going to take it anymore!" The anger serves as fuel to justify doing something completely different to shake up the system and the determination helps propel the person into action. The woman who made national news by going on strike when her family did not appreciate her certainly upped the ante.

Upping The Ante

Write down an intolerable situation you have been trying to change without success. _____

_____

Let your mind wander and see what options you could consider if the unacceptable behavior of the other person or the situation does not change. Make some of them funny and some serious. List at least five options.

_____

_____

_____

_____

Picture yourself carrying out the different alternatives. Get into a delicious fantasy of how you could take charge by living out your stated consequences. Visualize yourself standing firm on the position you have taken. See the stress that each alternative would create for you. Note your feelings about each one. Reject the alternatives that have to do with revenge and choose one where you feel very good about yourself. Choose the option that increases your self-esteem and write it here. _____

_____

_____

Now list reasons why your plan might not work. _____

_____

Who would get angry and apply pressure to you? List the external threats to you. _____

_____

_____

Visualize yourself standing up to the stress. See yourself really handling the consequences and the emotional feelings the stress might cause. How would you feel? How many days could you hold out? What actions could you take to handle the stress? _____

_____

_____

Determine if the consequence is worth taking. Are you willing to live with the results of your actions? Describe how your life would be different.

_____

_____

Now view yourself successfully handling your course of action. Write a sensational *National Enquirer* type headline to describe your victory!

_____

Fantasize the national attention from the media that would go hand in hand with your accomplishments. See yourself being interviewed on a talk show by Phil Donahue or Oprah Winfrey. How do you feel about the accomplishments you have achieved in your fantasy? _____ Only you can determine if you need to up the ante to bring about some desired changes in your life about a situation that is intolerable to you.

Becoming oneself is one of life's greatest achievements. Instead of wondering what others think about you, the question becomes, "How can I have positive regard for myself without an excessive need for external approval from others?" In the process of becoming autonomous, the myth of perfection begins to crumble. Reality means understanding that no one is perfect and our efforts to strive for perfection only end in frustration and self-defeat. You can invest your personal energy to learn that you do not have to be dogmatic in your shoulds, musts, have tos, oughts, commands, demands and compulsions. As you learn to change your language and use positive statements about yourself and others, you will view life differently. There will be greater expression of creativity and self-assertion as you grow in communication abilities and social skills. Competence as a mature individual can thus become positively accomplished.

SIX

Stumbling Blocks That Doormats Constantly Trip Over

If I knew for sure that a man was coming to my house with the conscious design of doing me good, I would run for my life.

Henry David Thoreau

The Give And Take Of Relationships

"What you see is what you get," comedian Flip Wilson tells us. More rightly so, "What you get is what you expect." Doormats can be caught up in a reduced or wrong set of expectations. They don't expect much for themselves, and, therefore, end up with very little. There are three basic questions that you can ask yourself concerning this issue. How do I expect to treat others? How do I expect others to treat me? However, the most important question is, "How do I treat myself?" The first two are based on the last; how you treat and are treated by others depends on how you treat yourself. When we learn to treat ourselves with love and respect, then it comes back to us in many measures. Somehow Doormats grow up learning to respect others more than themselves. When you truly learn the 3 R's — the three respects of valuing self, others and property — then your life will become more productive and harmonious.

All relationships are mutually advantageous or symbiotic in nature, being designed to meet the conscious and unconscious needs of both individuals. A symbiotic relationship of a destructive nature is similar to the mistletoe that is beautiful to look at and even can spark romance, but saps the strength out of a living organism. Partners can lean on each other to the extent that both are drained. As the song goes, it takes two to tango or even tangle. In pairing, one partner is generally submissive in one area while the other is dominant. Spoken and unspoken rules constitute the partnership and define how the individuals should act. One may have more of the say over the checkbook and decide how money is to be spent while the other has more say in another area.

In balanced relationships there is an equality of areas and neither person has undue power. However, in a co-dependent relationship, the system is on permanent tilt because the personality needs of both people cause them to focus on their unmet, unresolved needs. The all-too-forgiving nature of the Placator dovetails with the strong need-to-control nature of the Blamer or the refusal-to-look-at-it nature of the Super-Reasonable. Relationships are like governments. They need a natural system of checks and balances built into them lest one ruling faction run away with the power. If there is no righting mechanism because one partner always gives in, honest communication cannot develop. Extremes of co-dependent behavior can keep your relationship perpetually out of balance.

Relationships: Bargains And Otherwise

One way to look at your relationships is on a cost/benefit ratio. Put simply, are you getting back what you are putting into it? While it may seem hardhearted to apply an economic formula to people, it is a way to better understand how you allow yourself to be treated by others. Consider your interactions with your parent, partner, friend or child and ask yourself these heart-rending questions.

- Is what I'm getting worth the cost?
- Am I getting what I pay for?
- Am I willing to pay the cost for what I get?
- Do I get equal value for my effort, time and money?
- Am I giving up too much of my personal power?
- Does the relationship allow me to grow and learn?
- If it doesn't permit growth and learning, why not?

The key to understanding and learning about respect is the concept of "equal value." People may be in different roles or positions (worker/boss, parent/child, pupil/teacher, doctor/patient, wife/husband), but they still are of equal value. At any given time, one may be the expert, the decision maker or the one who is in charge, but the value of each as a human being is equal. You are not better or worse than others; you are not above or below them or they, you. With a working knowledge of the concept of equal value, your actions toward others will change greatly. All people will be treated the same with dignity and respect. Until you comprehend the depth of this concept and apply it daily to your life, you will continue with an unbalanced power mentality.

A Victim For All Seasons

We often grow up treating ourselves in the same way that our parents treated us. We love and accept ourselves and criticize ourselves in the same ways. Often we act out the relationship between our parents by creating it again and again. If one or both of your parents identified with the victim role, then you may have learned attitudes and beliefs that are similar. The victim role heavily invests in blame mentality that says, "Feel sorry for me because he (or she or they) did it to me." Blaming perpetuates the attitude of being a helpless victim.

Doormats spend some portion of each day feeling sorry for themselves. You may view yourself as a good person but believe terrible things happen to you that are outside of your control. Every time you do, you make it easier to think the same thought again. Brain research shows that thinking the same thing over and over creates well-worn pathways in the brain. Every time you experience the same thought, connections are formed between the synapses and the cells. These pathways become deeper when the thoughts are repeated, and it is probable that the same thought pattern will occur increasingly. Habitual ways of thinking have years of practice behind them, and powerful techniques are needed to change them.

The Poor Me Tally Sheet

How many times a day do you put yourself in the victim role? You may view yourself as a good person but terrible things happen to you that are beyond your control. With this "poor me" attitude you then feel justified in feeling sorry for yourself and in doing so, avoid the responsibility to make things better for yourself. If you catch yourself sighing a lot and feeling hopeless, check to see if this is related to underlying feelings of being a victim or a martyr.

This exercise asks you to look at how you spend precious time and energy in viewing yourself as a victim. People with a victim mentality have a set of internal negative statements they make over and over that contribute to their feeling bad. What is your typical phrase that signals your victimhood? How many times a day or a week do you substantiate your role as the victim with your phrase?

_____ Why me?
_____ Poor me. Things always happen to me.
_____ I don't deserve this.
_____ Why does God have to punish me this way?
_____ He or she or they are always doing things to cause me pain.
_____ It just isn't fair.
_____ Woe is me. Is life really worth it?

From whom did you learn this self-defeating way of thinking? List the real-life people that you have identified with who practiced victim behavior.

_____

What fictional victims in a novel, movie or television show are you

fascinated with? _____

Make a tally sheet of the number of times a day you say self-defeating statements. By constantly or even occasionally giving power to these negative statements, you draw further negative events into your life. Your choice to control your thoughts can become part of the solution rather than contributing to your feeling sorry for yourself. Do you gain attention from others when you complain about how bad you have it? What benefits have

you gained from being a martyr? _____

_____

How has this role been harmful to you? _____

_____

Close your eyes and view yourself in that well-known victim role. See yourself overwhelmed by outside forces over which you have no control. How do you feel about the helplessness you are experiencing? Let these forces take on an abstract shape or form. Ask your Inner Wisdom to let you have a moment of truth so that you can view yourself in a different way. Let your subconscious mind become a mirror for these forces so that you realize they are really of your own making. Allow the insight that your negative attitude has placed you in a position where others dump all over you. See how you determine your part in the situations that happen to you.

Stop and acknowledge how you are giving your power away to negative belief systems. Realize you do have choices in this area. Visualize yourself starting to take conscious control over the negative phrases that keep you in the martyr's role. When you hear yourself start to say a negative phrase, remember that you are responsible for every thought you create.

You may be a situational victim, but you need not be a psychological victim of someone else or your own faulty belief system. You may be caught in a situation that further contributes to your problems but you can change this. Stop playing victim and victimizer. Stop taking credit or blame. As you learn and grow, you can choose to leave a situation that is not good for you. You can mourn the situation and move on from it.

The current rash of books that blame men for women's problems ignores the symbiotic nature of relationships. This position allows women to avoid taking responsibility for themselves by putting energy into feeling wretched and angry instead of problem solving and doing something about the situation.

A more involved outlook would be to look at ways women could act differently in relationships rather than spending energy putting down men — who represent half of the human race — for their past behavior. If we must use the word victim, then think of it as, "We are victims of victims of victims." Today's people, both men and women, are the product of generational patterns of ignorance and abuse based on inequalities of power. Both sexes have been damaged by the injustices. Our world may have needed the feminist movement to publicize these inequalities but now we can move on from blaming men for women's problems. Now we are being given the chance to break out of the old ways of thinking and acting. The process of recovery, whether it is an individual or the world, is to move out of the victim/victimizer mentality and take responsibility for our own actions.

Taking Responsibility For Your Choices

Another obstacle on the road to recovery from co-dependency is allowing others to make choices for you. This is the "It doesn't matter" syndrome that stems from a fear of making the wrong decision. It can also come out of habit or old-fashioned laziness. This pattern is reflected by statements like:

- Well, what do **you** want to do?
- Anything is okay with me.
- I don't care.
- Whatever you say.
- It doesn't matter.

Sometimes it really doesn't matter which alternative you choose; alternative A is just as exciting as alternative B. When choices are of equal value to you, then it makes sense to let other people choose if they have a definite preference. But if you find yourself habitually avoiding decisions on a regular basis and letting other people choose for you, then watch out, it's Doormat time!

The real issue is avoiding responsibility when you let the other person make the decision. Not making a choice is choosing to be passive. Ambivalence can become a way of life that results in a tapioca pudding type of personality. Passivity dries up your juiciness. The ability to make decisions and follow through with the consequences is a learned skill with practice as the major necessary ingredient. If you don't practice making the little choices and learning from your mistakes, you will have trouble when it comes to the big ones.

If Nurturing Is Your True Nature, Watch Whom You Nurture

Another impediment to independent living is that Doormats are slow learners when it comes to self-care. They are experts at nurturing others but know little or nothing about nourishing and cherishing themselves. Because they have not learned to take care of themselves properly, they cannot take care of others in a way that is beneficial to both. If you don't nurture yourself, you may find that you become more and more resentful that no one notices how hard you are trying to hold things together. You may become exhausted and even burn out. Your body will let you know when you are not taking care of it properly. Doormats have a tendency to develop stress-related illnesses because they have internal rules that tell them to keep going even when they are worn out. So if you are feeling stressed because of the need to do for someone else, stop and take a second look. A major goal is for you to learn to nurture yourself more than you have been. If you feel more satisfied and appreciated, you can let go of some of that desire to take care of someone else.

Nurturing — Past And Present

Close your eyes and breathe deeply; allow yourself to drift back in time to examine how you have contributed to imbalance in your relationships by continually choosing to nurture the other person instead of yourself. Return now to a time early in your childhood when you first became consciously aware of taking care of other people. Let your memories carry you back through your lifetime; note others for whom you have felt responsible, the desperation you felt and the ways that you have tried to help them. Do not get caught up in any one situation; just note it and move on to the next. See yourself with an accumulation of co-dependent behavior over a lifetime. Write down the names of the important people you remember, a brief word or two about how you tried to take care of them and your feelings about the outcome.

Person	How You Nurtured	Your Emotional Response

What are your feelings as you complete this exercise about your history of ignoring your own needs? Do you feel angry, cheated, depleted or overwhelmed? _____

How do you feel about the feelings stated above as you examine your lifelong habits? _____

Did you become a little adult, all serious and responsible, and let go of that happy, spontaneous child? What parts of yourself did you give up as a little child? _____

What nurturing did you deny yourself to play the caretaker role? _____

_____

Now, bring yourself to the present and choose a person in a current relationship that you are intensely involved in trying to help. How are you overextending yourself to this person? _____

Does this person remind you of an earlier situation? Is this a more updated version of your trying to make it better for your mother, father or another member of your family? _____ How have you given up opportunities to take care of yourself by nurturing this other person? _____
In what ways have you deprived yourself because you had to do so much for another person? _____

As you reflect on this, what tension and discomfort are you experiencing in your body? _____

What stress-related illness do you have? _____
How has your peace of mind been affected through your worry and concern?

Describe how your spending excess time giving to the relationship has affected your self-esteem as well as the other person's _____

Write down the choices you could make regarding your own needs: _____

Now quietly and lovingly be responsive to those deeply felt needs that have long been denied. Know, really let yourself know, what your longings are regarding your need to be nurtured. From the most loving space within you, give yourself permission to have your own needs met for physical comfort, internal peace and emotional nourishment. Say to yourself, at least ten times a day, "I am a worthwhile person capable of getting what I need to be happy. I give myself permission to nourish and love myself. I give myself permission to be nourished and loved."

The "If Only" Syndrome

Another roadblock that prevents Doormats from acting in appropriate ways is that they believe in their own omnipotence. They sometimes believe that they are responsible for everything and the cause of everything, which is a symptom of grandiose thinking. Doormats can have high expectations for change and a need to control outcomes for other people. When something does not go the way they expect, the Doormat is ripe for feeling inadequate. They believe they are at fault because they did not help enough and get a bad case of thinking, "If only . . . ." "If only I had been stronger then . . . . If only I had thought of . . . . If only I had tried harder with . . . ." This grandiose thinking that you can fix someone else always hooks back into poor self-esteem. It takes a lot of personal energy to be in charge of the world or even your little part of it.

The root problem behind rescuing is that we are brought up to believe that others really can't stand on their own two feet. Doormats take the prerogative of taking care of people who are perfectly capable of taking care of themselves. They say, "Dear, the world out there is too hard for you. You'd better stay with me and let me handle it for you." This subtle message, "You are not strong enough to make it on your own," cripples and incapacitates the other person psychologically.

Sometimes the hardest accomplishment is to do nothing, and the best thing you can do for that other person is to learn to say the N-word — no. Yet by learning to say it, you can stop the anguish and the active hurting on behalf of another person. Here are some other things you can learn: Refrain from wanting to heal someone else. Stop being the enabler that slyly encourages other people to continue in their dysfunctional behavior. Stop demeaning both yourself and the other person by your worry and concern. Give other people the freedom to struggle creatively on their own. As the philosopher Nietzsche said, "For this is hardest of all: to close the open hand out of love."

Feeling Good About Saying The N-word To Someone Who Needs It

To reestablish yourself in a relationship you may have to establish your-self as an equal partner. That means learning to say the N-word. One statistic that would be interesting for you to note is the number of times you agree during the day. Take a tally of how many times you say yes and no. If you find that you are agreeing too much and taking a toll on your integrity, then you may want to reconsider what your choices really are. Who do you say yes to most of the time? Which people do you give in to automatically: your

mother, the boss, your spouse or one of your kids? _____
Write down a situation in your life where you are uncomfortable because you go along with conditions that do not fit for you so that you can help

another person who needs to learn to be self-sufficient. _____

Be in touch with your internal discomfort with the situation. Ask your Inner Wisdom for some guidance on how you should act in this situation. How

can you set your boundaries as to what is right for you? _____

_____

What do you need to say to the other people involved in the situation?

_____

How can you best say no? Be creative in your expression of stating your own needs. Here are some ideas for you.

- This just doesn't fit for me.
- It is wonderful to hear what you want, but it is not for me.
- Thank you for thinking of me, but I have other plans.
- No doesn't mean I hate you, it just means this is not right for me.
- My intuition (Inner Wisdom) tells me this isn't right for me.

Now choose how you would express your N-word in this situation. _____

_____

Practice saying it out loud. How does it feel to assert yourself in a mature, loving manner? Practice it again and again in all sorts of ways. Sing it, whisper it, shout it and say it in another language. Get used to the feel of saying no to those who really need to work things out on their own. Make a commitment to yourself to say no in situations that are right for you to do so. And feel good about saying yes to saying no!

❧ SEVEN ❧

Release From
Doormat Thinking

---

*We are what we think having become what we thought. And joy
follows a pure thought like a shadow faithfully tailing a man.*

Buddha
The Dhammapada

Crazy Things You Say To Yourself To Hold On To Co-dependency

There are some ways of thinking that will help you release yourself from
co-dependent behavior and thinking. A core belief about the dignity of
human beings that will help you see straight is that people do the best that
they know how with the psychological resources that are available to them.
People do not purposely plan to mess up their lives. People who are caught
in addictive behavior do so because they do not have other choices available
at that time. If people could do better, they would. This belief about the basic
integrity of people goes past blame into a humanistic outlook.

The issue to look at is acceptance. Accept the fact that all people on this
earth have the right to be who they are and make the choices they make. (If

you hear yourself arguing with this, check out your should-message!) Human beings are given equal opportunities for lessons and growth no matter what their station in life. Even if the choices are not to our liking or in other people's best interests, it is their life to do with as they choose. You may not like it, but that is how it is.

Accept that there is nothing you can do to **make** other people change. All you can do is change the way you act or react to them, or change how you regard others. The cleanest response you can make is to take care of you and let others take care of themselves.

Looking at these next roadblocks will focus on ways you may justify spending time and energy worrying about other people instead of being accountable to changes that are needed in your own behavior. Doormats sometimes get mired down by a phrase or two that are said over and over but have no real value. Continual use of these phrases only adds to getting caught up in the resignation of the situation. These phrases include, "He's not living up to his potential," "But I feel so sorry for him," and "It's for his own good."

You always hurt the one you love, as the popular song goes, but **for sure** this is true when you try to take care of the other person's problems. One brick that some Doormats put in front of themselves to trip over is getting caught up in the concept of potential. Parents of children who do not do well can spend a lifetime agonizing because "They're not living up to their potential!" This attitude may start in grade school and becomes stronger in junior high when students fail due to poor motivation even though they may be bright. Parents become angry and despair when they can't make their children do well in their studies. Recriminations and tension in the household set the stage for children to fail further. Parents may gripe about their children to others and set up stringent guidelines for becoming overly involved in homework. Children learn that they can gain attention and power by not doing well and develop passive-aggressive behavior. If the anguish and anger of the parents go unchecked, young people can grow up hanging onto their motivational pattern of failing in life. The self-fulfilling prophecy of "not living up to their potential" becomes a reality as a result of co-dependent control.

Childhood is the training ground for learning necessary skills for independence. When you take over responsibilities for your children that they are perfectly capable of doing, you rob them of valuable lessons that they need to learn. Childhood is the time when children must try out many roles to practice how they will act as adults. They need to fail at some of the things they do so that they can learn the skills of dealing with failure. They benefit from experiencing the consequences of their choices and actions, both positive and negative, as they grow to independence and maturity. As parents, our major job is to gradually step back as authority figures so our children learn to stand on their own two feet and "right" themselves when they find they are off balance, or pick themselves up when they fall on their faces!

A helpful guideline in dealing with both children and adults is the principle of error correction. Error correction is the practice of using corrective feedback, without any hint of judgment. Feedback is given about the behavior for the purpose of correcting the error, not to scold, criticize or punish the person. Mistakes are made to be fixed. That is why pencils have erasers. Errors are learnings that have yet to emerge. Error making is part of the evolutionary process in both the survival of the species and in the individual man or woman. People are presented with experiences both positive and negative to which they can apply new learnings. The old way of thinking and acting becomes a stepping stone to new possibilities when negative judgment and emotions are not present. In the struggle to find meaning behind misfortune and trauma, corrections of dysfunctional patterns can emerge. Sometimes we may even commit the error so that it can be worked through!

The beauty of the error correction approach to life is that it does away with the concept of blame. It provides a no blame/no shame framework for problem solving. Blaming others or yourself is a waste of time and only leads to increasing the resistance to change. When children are raised with the approach that they can make mistakes but are expected to learn from them, the pressure of not to fail is removed. Failure can be defined as the way to success in that it will take you where you need to go if you learn from it. Positive self-esteem does not depend on being perfect but from cleaning up one's act. Learning from the situation and correcting it creates an optimistic, pragmatic, as well as a loving, gentle approach to treating yourself and others.

Doormats often display a high degree of pity for the misfortunes of other people because they have been raised to feel guilty much of the time. They have not learned productive ways of dealing with the pain of others. They have been brought up with the notion that the way to help people is to feel sorry for them and/or rescue them. They feel bad because there is an internal "should" that says, "People should not experience pain. I should feel sorry for anyone who is in pain." With their high degree of guilt, the internal unconscious reasoning is, "He hurts; I don't; therefore, I should feel bad." This attitude weighs both sender and recipient down because it taps into shame. This is brought about by a misunderstanding of the nature and value that pain plays. Giving with the open heart without being drawn into the sadness of the other person is reflected in the words of the Sufi spiritual teacher, Reshad Field, in *The Invisible Way:*

> *Do not be sentimental about discomfort . . . sentimental-*
> *ity can be the greatest enemy of love. The pain I have is*
> *mine; it is not yours. You have your own to deal with,*
> *whether physical or emotional. You cannot help me with*
> *the pain . . . you can be sympathetic but please don't*
> *identify. Never identify yourself with anything, not your*
> *own so-called problems, not those of another. Be yourself*
> *at all times.*

Pain is merely an indication that there is something that needs correcting. As Kahlil Gibran said in his famous book, *The Prophet,* "Your pain is the breaking of the shell that encloses your understanding." The pain that accompanies an infection indicates that healing needs to take place. The pain that is present during a loss, such as divorce or death, means that the person is adjusting to the loss. Serious illness can allow the opportunity to reassess what is of paramount value. Through suffering, we are presented with valuable lessons on how to live our life in a more satisfying manner by releasing that which is detrimental to us. Pain presents an opportunity to look at the situation differently and make different choices whether it be changes in diet, in lifestyle or in our treatment of ourselves or others.

Pity is a learned way of dealing with other people's traumas in a misguided attempt to share their pain. Pity arises from a feeling of guilt and a sense of lack in the individual. It is based in the ego and has the noble intent to correct situations, but uses the means of devaluing the other individual. It is nonproductive for both parties involved. We all have had many guilt messages taught to us about how we should think and act when faced with someone who is less fortunate than we are. Compassion is the ability to care for others and help them without feeling their pain. As human beings we are obliged to live a life of loving and sharing with others. The triumph of compassion over pity allows people their dignity and wholeness even at their time of trial. As we grow spiritually, we learn to make the fine discernment between pity and compassion.

Another obstacle to the development of mature relationships is the tendency for Doormats to stick their noses in other people's business. They have nose attacks of knowing what is best for others and find ways to tell them about it. This is your basic meddling that comes in small, medium and large sizes. Doormats seem to be allergic to MYOB (minding your own business). They have some belief systems that stimulate, irritate and aggravate those parts of the brain that say, "You're not a good person unless you get off your duff and go over there and help someone." This belief is a major stumbling block because if you stick your nose where it doesn't belong, you may not watch where you are going, you may trip and fall down a lot, or you may lose sight of your own vision in trying to pave the way for someone else.

It is easy to justify meddling behavior on the grounds that "it's for their own good." Engaging in this thought time and again keeps individuals bound up in negative energy. "For their own good" is another version of a power trip. It comes from a controlling mind-set that says, "I know better than anyone else what is best for them." It means to do your will and not allow others to work things out on their own. It is often enlisted for your convenience and peace of mind to rationalize your action against other people.

Giving up control over other people can be accomplished by looking at the "shoulds" that you have tucked away for them. What "shoulds" for other people are you clinging to in the guise of helping?

- You should express your feelings.
- You should stop . . . .
- You should make better grades.
- You should straighten up your life.
- You should get a job.
- You should . . . .

When you practice the "shoulds" for other people, your judgmental self has determined how conditions must be. Trying to control by worrying and knowing what is best for others means holding on to negative energy. This energy behind your expectation provides a contagious effect, which blocks beneficial change. With your negative belief system you are both fixed in a pattern of behavior that cannot be liberated. In releasing other people from your beliefs on how they should be, you discharge that energy. In releasing the judgment and expectation, you may set free their symptoms. Loving acceptance of others can balance all. The ancient Chinese philosophy of Lao Tzu from the *Tao-te Ching* tells us: "I take no action and the people are transformed of themselves; I prefer stillness and the people are rectified of themselves; I am not meddlesome and the people prosper of themselves. I am free from desire and the people of themselves become simple like the uncarved block."

Letting go of the anxiety you feel when other people do not do well is a skill you can learn if you faithfully work on your attitudes, belief systems, phrases and behavior. As Satir said, "Give people your hand but not your back." Tough love is doing what you know is right and being willing to live with the consequences. Becoming comfortable with the "come what may" of the natural consequences is a way for you to give other people back their own power. Vernon Howard, the author of *The Powers Of Your Supermind,* tells it like this: "Please don't go around trying to save the world. You have all you can do to save yourself. Begin by seeing that something in you needs correction. That is a perfect start."

Putting An End To A Meddling Attack

To help you give others the gift of your noninterference, choose a person and a specific situation for your withdrawal exercise. Visualize the person in the typical behavior that you find objectionable. Now take a rational look at your own behavior. Are you about to have a compulsive attack of meddling? If you are aching to set someone straight, then it is probably an outbreak of Doormat time. **Stop! Wait!** Breathe deeply and continue your visualization while considering the implications of your involvement. Ask yourself the following questions:

Why have you assigned yourself as a keeper of another human being? ____

____

How are you and this person enmeshed in a nonproductive clash of wills?

____

Describe how your actions set off passive-aggressive behavior in the other

person's reactions. ____

How has your enabling made the other more resistant to looking at the

problem? ____

Has your involvement put distance and secrecy between you? ____

____

How is the person expressing resentment because of your interference?

____

Is the other person promising to change but not living up to the prom-

ises? ____

Has it brought about short-term change and a honeymoon period, then back

to business as usual? ____

What secret resentments do you harbor because the person is not changing

the way you expected? ____

What setbacks have happened as a result of your interference? ____

____

How do you want to see yourself in this matter? ____

Get in touch with how you would like to be. Would you rather have control or peace of mind? What role is in your best interest as well as that of the

other person? ____

What type of person do you long to be? _____
How would you feel if you would allow yourself to become who you want

to be? _____

Over the years you have developed your caring part very well. Now you are learning to add the withholding part. Are you ready to let go of your enabling so that others can learn to take responsibility for themselves? Visualize yourself stating your concern lovingly to another person while telling this person you must pull back from your overly helpful ways.

Now realize the value of the gift that you are offering this person you care so deeply about. You are giving this person the opportunity for growth. Others may not choose to take your gift of offered growth, but that is their prerogative. You are allowing them the freedom to struggle creatively on their own. Tell them how hard this is for you to do. For the first time see that you really can let others take responsibility for their own actions so that they may learn self-respect. How does it feel for you to do this? Finish the sen-

tence, When I _____, I

feel _____.

It really is all right for you to release your responsibility for this person. Tell yourself this statement over and over again until you know the truth that it holds for you. If this exercise is hard for you because you can't let go of the pain and anxiety you feel for another person, then you may need to reread some of the chapters and rework some of the exercises.

The biggest stumbling block of all in co-dependency is false pride. It will trip you every time and you'll fall flat on your face. Pride is self-glorification and self-importance; it is pretension and vanity. It is presuming that you know better than anyone else the right way to do things. It coaxes you to try to put your standards in someone else's head. In doing so, you feel justified, but it is an insult to the other person. False pride, in this sense, is that need to feel superior to someone else. It puffs you up like a toad but it's all hot air.

Excessive pride goes back to that stubborn, little child who digs in its heels, folds its hands across its chest and says, "Hell, no. You can't make me. I'm going to do it my way. You do it my way too." It is that passive-aggressive part of ourselves that will not let anyone else tell us what to do even as we hurt ourselves in the process. Except in this instance, it is not a parent or another person trying to change us; we are being nudged by our own Higher Self to look at ourself in a new way.

Discovering that you are arrogant about your need to have people do things your way is just another challenge for growth. Learning about it will help you become honest about why you feel the need to change people. It is simply another coping mechanism you have learned to help you deal with stress. Retreating to the position of superiority is a distancing stance shown in Super-Reasonable behavior. The other side of the coin of false pride is humility, which is a very exciting journey to travel.

Letting Go — Letting God

Letting go is what this is all about, folks. The 12-Step programs speak of the wisdom of letting your Higher Power handle those issues that are disruptive in your life. As you are in the process of recovery from co-dependency, so are your significant others in their own unique process of what they are becoming. Trust that their process will take them where they need to go even though they may have to hit bottom first. Find the professional help that is needed for them, but more importantly, find it for yourself. Trust that what needs to happen to them will happen. Lay down the burden of your expectations of how things must be for them. Lay down that yoke of control. Release that negative energy that binds you together; in doing so you allow the power of others to unfold.

The scriptures of all religious traditions tell us that we are to be of a generous nature and open heart. We are our brothers' keepers but we can learn ways to do so that do not cripple them. A keeper in the old sense of the word meant a jailer, custodian or warden. We can truly become our brothers' keepers by keeping their spirits intact. We can give other people the tools they need so that they can help themselves. This means not depriving others of their struggle by helping them. This also requires not insulting people by doing for them what they can do for themselves. Examine your attitudes regarding struggle and pain. Allowing others their right to struggle and meet their problem head on is one of the best gifts that you can give.

In being open to the concept of our brothers' keepers, we must remember to be our own keeper as well. The danger in Doormat behavior is that you can easily become depleted through your efforts in meeting the perceived needs of others. If you don't have it to give, then you can't give it away. Double drowning is when you try to rescue someone and end up being pulled under yourself. After all, who rescues the rescuer? Who takes care of the caretaker?

What You Did Is Very Nice, But Is It Co-dependency?

How do you know when you are engaging in behavior that is nonproductive for you and the other person? Alcoholics Anonymous suggests that you use the HALT formula. This says not to make any decisions when you are *H*ungry, *A*ngry, *L*onely or *T*ired. Some other guidelines to use to determine if your behavior is co-dependent in nature are:

1. Is the other person asking for advice or your help? Or are you offering unsolicited opinions and suggestions?
2. What is your intent and motivation? Is there any element of trying to control other people? Do you "know" what is best for them? Are you fulfilling a need to be the expert?
3. Are you doing for them what they need to be doing for themselves? Are you bailing them out in any way? Are you preventing them from learning a much needed consequence?
4. What emotional state are you in at the time? Are you upset, angry or anxious? Are you acting out of fear or guilt? Co-dependent behavior is more likely to occur when you are in an emotional state of mind.
5. What is your physical state at the time? Are you fatigued, harried or overwrought? Be aware that if you do not have the physical energy to help at the time but do it anyway, then you are not acting in your own best interest. If you go ahead and do it anyway, then you are probably practicing co-dependency.
6. What is your attachment to the outcome? Are you desperately trying to promote change? The more emotionally involved and attached you are, watch out.
7. What "should" rule are you operating under? The total dynamics of the situation calls for your action, not your survival rules, guilt or anxiety. The situation is defined by all of the guidelines just mentioned.
8. Give it the "fit test." Does what you are about to do fit for you? Does it feel good? Be really honest with yourself. What does your intuition tell you about your proposed action? Tune in and listen!
9. If you can say sincerely to yourself, "I choose this action because it is in my best interest as well as that of the other person," then you are safe. If your action is congruent with your Inner Wisdom, then it is right for you.

To cease rescuing and placating doesn't mean that you have to stop being a generous person. The essential difference is to make the decision to do something for others out of the goodness of your heart rather than out of your neurotic needs. It may also signify that it is appropriate for the other people to refuse what is being offered. In your enlightened state you realize that what fits for you may not fit for them, and that is perfectly all right. This may also imply waiting to be asked before jumping in and offering (otherwise known as sitting on it). Sometimes this may indicate that you will literally have to bite your tongue to keep from speaking!

You can use hindsight to become more knowledgeable about similar acts in the future. Often actions can best be looked at by examining your internal reaction after the act is finished. If you experience physical discomfort, such as a nervous stomach, tight shoulders or other tension in your body, then you might question the wisdom of your action. Emotional reactions to be aware of include anger, worry, unhappiness, guilt or relief. You may be overly pleased with yourself indicating that you are still "hooked on" enabling.

You may not always be able to make a clear cut decision on the burning issue, "Is this Doormat behavior or not?" But with these guidelines in mind, you will be aware of the traps you set for yourself. You can make conscious decisions rather than always operating from your murky subconscious. Now and then you may fall unwittingly into some semi-Doormat behavior. But if you slip up, remember to be loving and forgiving to yourself because your errors are a source for further learning.

There will be a noticeable difference in your relationships as you clean up your co-dependency act. As you learn more and more, you will find yourself backing off from situations that you previously would have relished. You may even go through a period of selfishness as you swing to the opposite pole. No matter. If you keep in touch with your loving nature and continue to develop your Inner Wisdom, you will find a happy medium.

You may find old friends dropping away now that you take more responsibility for your behavior and expect them to take care of themselves. You may refuse to let new people who send signals of being needy into your life. Certain family members may become more distant now that you are no longer enmeshed in their pain and dysfunctional behavior. Unnecessary relationships and their hold on you will fall by the wayside. The exciting part is that you will attract friendships that are more mature. The flavor of your life gets better as you grow in maturity and self-understanding..

Moving Out Of Doormat City

Changes are happening in male-female relationships as publicity is given to self-created barriers to intimacy and equality that exist. Recent surveys show that men and women are finding that they have other choices than to stay in relationships where they are unhappy. Women in dysfunctional marriages who earn their own paychecks find that the pluses of social approval and financial security of marriage no longer apply. Men who have shouldered excessive responsibility all of their lives are beginning to look for ways of taking care of themselves. People with co-dependent tendencies are learning new skills and are beginning to stand up for their rights within their relationships. As the saying goes, "Times, they are a-changing!"

Pulling back from co-dependency does not require that you stop giving support to others. You can maintain a relationship with them if you state your feelings honestly when you are concerned about what they are doing. You can encourage them to go into therapy, a treatment center or self-help group. You can encourage them rather than enable them by saying again and again that they have the ability to do what they need to do to bring about positive changes on their own behalf. Then step back and leave them to it. If they refuse to change, then your responsibility is to take care of your own behavior.

Release from a lifetime of being overly involved with others means learning to set aside your own overzealous need to heal. Release and recovery from co-dependency depend on your ability to let other people heal themselves even though they have to go through hell to do it. It means to stop feeling the personal anguish that belongs to others. You must stand back and let them experience the natural consequences of their behavior. This means to stop living the lie that says, "I am fixed if I can fix another human being."

When you learn to be primarily accountable to yourself, the stage is set for other people to have more choices. They may choose to accept responsibility and take care of themselves or they may find others to take care of them in the way that you used to. Relationships will certainly change and there are no formulas to predict which way they will go. Your recovery means letting them live with the choices they make, even though they are upsetting to you. Then you will be free to take up the celebration of your own life.

As you move from a model of enabling to a model of empowering, you will discover great gifts in store for you. The greatest gift that you can give other people is your own well-being. Another gift is to allow them to be themselves even with all the shortcomings. Martin Buber, the great Jewish philosopher, put it well when he said, "Love is caring enough to take the sometimes painful responsibility of letting the other person be who they are."

🐾 EIGHT 🐾

Power, Addictions And The Sense Of Betrayal

The goal is to be as fully human as we can possibly be . . . when we are in touch with our personal power, we are in touch with our Divinity.

Virginia Satir

Giving Away Your Power

One way to give away power is to get caught in a pattern of destructive addictive behavior. The paradox is that people use addictive substances in an attempt to feel powerful. All addictions have a spiritual basis. They result when individuals seek to fill that which is missing in themselves with an external source, be it a substance, habit, activity or another person. It is an attempt to complement the self by turning to something that is outside for validation rather than expressing the true yearning to merge with the oneness of the universe.

Once upon a time the word addiction meant a dependence on alcohol or drugs. Today the term has a wider connotation and applies to a wide range of compulsive behaviors from "pigging out" on chocolate to escaping daily reality by reading romance novels. Addiction is compulsive negative behavior that functions as a coping mechanism to deal with stress, pain or depression. Currently, researchers are identifying the physiological basis of addictions by defining it as self-initiated problem behavior that brings about biochemical changes in the brain and provides temporary relief from stress. The bottom line may be an addiction to feeling good that is sustained by whatever substance or activity produces adrenalin in the body. This brings about changes in the neurotransmitters in the synapses in the brain cells to create a temporary sense of well-being. The adrenalin rush that addictive behaviors produce is also a powerful chemical. Perhaps co-dependents become hooked on their own hormonal changes and adrenalin produced by the high and withdrawals similar to drug or alcohol addiction.

Power, work and money addictions can take over a person's life as can the more well-known addictions of gambling and chemical dependence. Mood-altering behaviors (jogging or binge eating) and high-risk actions (sky diving or mountain climbing) qualify as addictions, as well as everyday activities (workaholism). But the short-lived fix is followed by a negative emotional state and the pain of withdrawal that leads to another bout with the addictive substance or activity to feel good. Thus, we are back to dysfunctional lifestyles and low self-regard as we seek relief from pain.

"Everything in moderation," the ancient philosophers wisely told us. Even religion has been termed an addiction if it is used obsessively with the exclusion of everything else to cope with life's stresses. Father Leo Booth, an Episcopalian priest working in the field of alcoholism, compares obsessive religious faith to drug addiction when it is used to escape reality. Some religions use strong methods to control their flock through the use of guilt and fear techniques such as threat of damnation. These practices increase an overdependence on the church authority. Ego power needs on the part of those in charge may approximate those of the benevolent dictator, but they foster dependence just the same. Many churches teach co-dependency as a way of life as a means of keeping people in line. People who have come from a religious upbringing that stresses sin and an inordinate number of rules (shoulds) often suffer from an unusual amount of guilt and likewise co-dependent behavior.

Even emotional states can become addictions. Suffering can become addictive due to the payoffs that it can produce. Suffering is the emotional reaction of holding onto pain. The continual pattern of falling in love to produce emotional highs and escape the humdrum quality of life is an addiction. Psychologists Harvey Milkman and Stanley Sunderwirth in their book *Craving For Ecstasy* describe people who are "romance junkies," using new relationships as a way of escaping feelings of inadequacy. Like the popular song, they are "Addicted to Love." They seek the euphoric state and adrenalin highs that accompany the finding of a new partner. They may have a psychological dependence on the temporary altered mood that a new and exciting partner brings. Men and women who are caught in such destructive relationships may be addicted to the same pattern of obtaining highs through their conflictual interactions with each other.

Co-dependency can be an addiction in the popular sense of romantic love. Co-dependent people distract themselves from their pain by getting high on their relationship with another person. This results from a deep need to blend and merge with something external, to gain comfort and well-being from another person, instead of from one's own self. Because of the incompleteness and sense of lack felt within, and the poor coping and communication skills, the co-dependent person cannot help but be drawn into destructive patterns of behavior from the past.

Serious negative addictions always separate you from others. The intensity of your need will push others away from you as they will need to protect themselves from your negativity. Completion by another substance, activity or person is the biggest delusion of all. Objects, substances, activities and other people do not complete us. We complete ourselves by becoming who we truly are.

As work in the co-dependency field becomes well-known, more and more people are discovering that this syndrome fits part or a substantial amount of their behavior. People who abuse alcohol or other substances may find that co-dependency underlies their addiction. In addition to their chemical dependency, they may also be cross-addicted to rescuing behaviors and suffer from the same lack of self-esteem. In some cases, the pressures of taking care of other people, and having poor coping skills and low self-esteem may lead to the second addiction of alcohol or drugs.

Some workers in the field of substance abuse have the belief that **all addictions are bad** and should be eliminated. "Get off your addictions," is their premise. This belief ignores basic human nature that seeks pleasure and avoids pain. In reality we seek those endorphins produced by the brain that promote that sense of well-being. We are biochemical creatures responding to our physiological nature.

Perhaps a better premise would be to change your addictions! It is important to make a distinction between negative and positive addictions. Negative addictions are rooted in lack of self-worth and love. They provide temporary relief from the pain of despair and allow periods of respite before the need settles in again. They emphasize short-term gratification with the hope that circumstances will somehow be different. The accompanying pattern of withdrawal, anxiety, guilt and discomfort can only be relieved by continuing the addiction. Negative addictions diminish people's sense of control and excitement about life as they further depreciate self-worth.

In his book *Positive Addictions,* William Glasser tells of healthy activities that can provide the same mood-altering brain chemistry without harm to the person. Positive addictions are those that are free or cheap, and are readily available or always with you. They allow you to feel both good and good about yourself. They enhance your ability to be more creative and effective at work. They add to the quality of your life and promote growth and expansion. And they are neither illegal, immoral nor fattening, which leaves out chocolate!

Positive addictions include meditation, gardening, sewing, journal keeping, woodworking and other creative acts that require a focusing of the mind to provide a respite from the daily problems while engaging in something pleasurable. Exercise, eating, reading or TV watching of a nonobsessive nature can also be a means of obtaining temporary relief from problems at hand. However, positive addictions do not take over and run your life and do not bring about a decrease in self-esteem. One of the most exciting positive addictions is taking charge of what happens to you and learning new coping strategies to deal with stress. Learning meaningful new ways of thinking and acting to promote self-growth can be one of the most productive of the positive addictions!

Identifying Your Addictions

From where do you obtain your comfort? _____

_____ This is your addiction.

Where do you place your meaning? _____

_____ This is your addiction.

Whom or what do you think about obsessively? _____

_____ This is your addiction.

When you are frightened, to whom or to what do you turn? _____

_____ This is your addiction.

When you are lonely and hurting, where do you go or what do you do to

obtain relief? _____

_____ This, too, is your addiction.

Now simply and lovingly assess what you have identified as the sources of your addictive behavior. Which ones sap your energy and draw you away from your True Self? Determine which factors are self-destructive and erode

self-esteem. _____

These are your negative addictions.

Which behaviors provide that sense of well-being and peace in your life? Which ones enhance who you are by becoming a pleasant pastime fostering relaxation, but do not fall within that out-of-control, destructive category? Which ones are preferences rather than necessities? Which ones help you become more truly who you are?

_____

These are your positive addictions.

Acknowledge what you have learned about yourself and which ways you have sought meaning and comfort. Do not fall into the trap of guilt or shame because you have a negative, addictive part of you, but simply be aware of the choices you have made up until now. This is simply where you are. It is not where you have to stay. You can learn to make wise choices that will empower you. Responsibility is understanding that you have put yourself in the situation because of your beliefs and choices. You can take yourself out of this unpleasant situation when you discover new beliefs and make new choices.

Jacqueline Small, in her book *Transformers: The Therapists Of The Future,* describes the gifts that negative addictions can hold because they are potential areas for growth. She says that because you know well the dark side of your nature, you can transform this knowledge into positive energy. The greatest sinner can become the greatest saint. Because you know the craving for alcohol or drugs, you have within the great longing for self-actualization. Because you have had the yearning for another person's love, you have the ability to love yourself. If you have given away your power, you now have a unique understanding of power and can claim it as your own. Through your addictions and the process of understanding them, you can make the choice to create your own positive future.

In And Out Of Love — In And Out Of Balance

Understanding addictions helps you understand how your emotions get out of control in relationships. One of the major tasks in life is to learn to balance the emotions. Karen Horney, an early psychoanalyst and theorist in the study of women, outlined three major categories of people who were out of balance in their relationships with others. She defined them in terms of their actions and movements. These categories are stereotypes and represent extremes in behavior, but they portray types of personalities to help understand the needs that cause individuals to choose partners.

The Detached

The *Detached* people among us move away from others and avoid intimate contact. They deny their emotions, and their need for love and friendships with other people. Intimacy and closeness are equated with being stifled. If their partner is perceived as being needy, they view it as too much of a demand and withdraw even more. They try to be self-reliant so that dependence on others is not needed. They wear a "Do not disturb" sign around their·necks to ward off people who try to get too close.

The Aggression Prone

The *Aggression Prone* people are those who move against others. They believe that others are incompetent and must be protected against themselves. They try to control weak-minded people who provide a reminder about what they really dislike about themselves. They believe in the survival of the fittest, and the world is seen as a hostile, threatening place where they must fight to survive. They tend to respond to people as tools that are to be used and use anger to keep others from getting too close. They repress any feelings of helplessness; in giving up their vulnerability, they give up their need for love. Their sign says, "Go ahead, make my day!"

The Helpless

The third type described by Horney is the *Helpless.* They too are out of balance because they repress healthy self-assertion and normal selfishness. They move toward others, and become overcompliant to the wishes and wants of those around them. They become the perpetual peacemakers, keeping the peace at any cost to themselves because they are frightened of conflict and argument. They become the Edith Bunkers of the world trying to overcome inner weakness by overexpressing care and concern for others. Their sign is worn on the you know where and says, "Kick me." The Helpless types are the typical Doormats and tend to join with the other two types so that they can get their needs for overcompliance met.

When the helpless type enters into a relationship with an aggressive person, the natural balance of power in the relationship is disturbed and the pattern for violence is set. Violence and aggression are learned patterns of behavior. Research shows that 75 percent of the batterers and 50 percent of the victims saw or experienced violence when they were children. The issue revolves around one partner trying to maintain absolute control, having learned as a child that aggression is an effective means of dealing with anger and feelings of poor self-esteem.

Cycle Of Violence

One hypothesis is that domestic violence may also have a physiological basis along with the emotional and psychological aspects. The *cycle of violence* has three stages.

Tension-Building Phase

In the *tension-building phase,* the man who is prone to temper outbursts is caught in unresolved power needs. When stress builds up, he may resort to drinking, which lowers his inhibitions.

Explosion Phase

The second phase is *explosion* where he takes out his violence on his wife verbally, sexually and physically. During aggressive acts, he may experience an adrenalin rush and an emotional high. This reaction causes physiological changes in his brain that are pleasant on a temporary basis. Later he may feel remorse and reduced self-esteem for going against society's standards. He tries to make up for his violence by being nice to his partner.

Honeymoon Period

This *honeymoon period* that is prevalent in the battered-wife syndrome may be accompanied in some men with guilt and remorse. Other men do not feel remorse, believing that the woman brought on the violence by her disobedience. The man may justify his actions by blaming his wife or pressures in society, and refuse to take responsibility for his own behavior. He will not seek help until he is forced to do so through court procedures.

Cycle Of Despair And Hope

The woman, who places high emphasis on love and romance, is caught in a cycle of despair and hope that dovetails with the man's behavior. Her low self-esteem becomes even more eroded during the violence stage. During the honeymoon period she may experience hope and believe that things will change. If she has been brought up in a family with a pattern of "Let's fight so we can make up," she may subconsciously provoke an incident.

The battered wife may remain in a violent situation because it is all she knows. In extreme cases, she, like the man, can become hooked on a cycle of lows and adrenalin highs that are similar to those of the addictive process. As the violence escalates, her internal state becomes so intensely caught in fear that she becomes immobile. Her immune system can become depressed, leaving her with little or no energy to make decisions. Her feedback system and ability to make choices becomes altered. The extreme fear that she experiences is real and is based on past experiences. A woman in this position may find it hard to leave because of the emotional and financial ties, and her fears of further violence. When she does leave and if she does not recover her self-esteem, she may re-create the same situation in a new relationship.

Unless the cycle is interrupted, the cycle will increase in aggressive behavior and encompass all family members. As long as the woman plays the role of protecting the man with denial of the problem and silence, violence will continue. It escalates in three major areas: verbal, physical and sexual; if not checked, it can end in death, suicide or rape.

Severe Patterns Of Behavior

There are two patterns of behavior that are so severe that people give away all of their power. These patterns are extreme enough that they are given psychiatric labels in the *Diagnostic And Statistical Manual — Revised,* a classification system used by psychiatrists and psychologists to diagnose mental disorders.

Dependent Personality Disorder

One pattern that requires treatment is *Dependent Personality Disorder.* Passivity, lack of self-confidence and the need for someone else to make personal decisions are the major descriptors of this disorder. These people feel uncomfortable and helpless when left alone. Because of ever-present fears of abandonment, they act in unpleasant, demeaning ways to win the approval of others. They feel inferior and use self-deprecating statements. They are devastated when a relationship ends. Because they cannot make decisions on their own, they seek out others who will dominate them. This pattern is learned when children are not allowed to speak for themselves and are kept dependent on the parents. When children grow up, they transfer this pattern of dependency to other people.

Self-Defeating Personality Disorder

A rarer type of disorder is seen in those people who seek out exploitive, abusive partners who are bad for them. This is a pervasive pattern of self-defeating behavior based on unconscious needs that began in childhood. The *Diagnostic and Statistical Manual — Revised* has proposed a new label of *Self-Defeating Personality Disorder* for this extreme pattern of behavior. Individuals with this type of disorder repeatedly get themselves into situations that are destructive even when better alternatives are available. They do not seem to be able to obtain pleasurable relationships and activities but instead seek out people and situations that lead to disappointment, failure and mistreatment. They cannot accept help, and people who are kind and caring are seen as boring. Any attempts on the part of others to make the situation better are sabotaged. These people must seek out abusive partners who provide the necessary excitement and stimulation that have been learned in childhood. There may be obsessive, excessive self-sacrifice that does not bring pleasure. Background factors in this personality disorder include having been physically, sexually or psychologically abused as children, or having been raised in a family where a parent was abused. In effect, these individuals are trying to re-create the conditions that are familiar from childhood. This is different from most types of co-dependency because it is an extreme pattern of behavior that must meet specific criteria before a diagnosis can be made.

The Dependent and the Self-Defeating Personality Disorders are extremes of behavior and are rare. They are different from the garden variety co-dependency. They should only be diagnosed by a clinician trained in looking at personality factors. Do not diagnose your friends or yourself with these labels. If you do see patterns of your behavior that might fit the descriptions of either one of these disorders, then it might be wise to check with a professional in the mental health field. Stop, do not pass go or collect the $200, but go directly to treatment! Be aware that help is available.

Releasing The Betrayal

People who give away their power often experience a strong sense of betrayal. This exercise will help you confront those feelings of betrayal as you get in touch with your lost innocence. Close your eyes and get in touch with some old memories in a safe way. Ask your Inner Wisdom to let you view only that which is comfortable for you to handle at this time. Look at the tiny child that you were who took on your parent's pain in an attempt to make conditions right in the family. Remember how you felt that you could never do enough to fix what was wrong in your mother or father. See how hard you tried and how you felt betrayed because no one gave you the credit you deserved. Remember the times when no one noticed and appreciated your hard work. Gently now, allow yourself to be aware of the anger that you felt at the sense of your betrayal. Anger is the pain that circled your innocence.

Now be aware of the person that did not live up to your expectations. This is not an exercise in blame — do not get carried away with anger. Just be aware of the information that you need to release some of the buried emotions. See your parents' helplessness and selfishness. See how they were caught in their own needs and were unable to care for you. Caught in their own pattern of dysfunction, which was learned in part from their own parents, they did the only thing that they knew how to do. Their pattern of behavior was predictable based on their lack of personal resources. Their unfair dealings and selfish behavior were their way of protecting their territory. Do not make a judgment here. Just understand what internal and external forces set up the circumstances into which you happened to be born.

Now be aware of you in that system. Go back in time to when you made the decision to take care of someone who was hurting. How old were

you? _____ What was the situation? _____

_____

What decision did you make? _____

_____

Who were you trying to protect? _____

_____

What did you have to do to take care of the other person? _____

_____

What compromises did you make regarding your needs? _____

_____

What coping mechanisms did you adopt to deal with the unhappiness in

your family? _____

_____

What messages did you learn about hurting? _____

_____

Did you take on any pain of the person you were protecting? ——————

——————————————————————————————————

How did you manifest that pain in your body? ————————————

——————————————————————————————————

Now for the very first time, see how things really were. See how you gave up your little child self while at the same time giving up your power to be you. See your betrayal of yourself. You did only what you could at that time with what resources that you had then. You could do no differently, just as your parents could do no differently. We all do the best that we can at the moment. Accept this as fact without judging it as bad or good. That is how things were. This was your family and this was your history. You cannot change your past but you can change your perception of it, and resolve to learn from what happened to you and how you chose to react.

Know now, deep in your heart, that conditions can be different from this time forward. Give yourself thanks for coming this far in understanding why you are the way you are and in deciding to do something about it. If you have not already done so, in time you can learn release by forgiving your parents and your little child for being caught in the misuse of power. You can now choose to regain your sense of self so that you can achieve personal power and self-sufficiency.

Social Competency

So much of who you are and how you present yourself to the world is related to what you believe about yourself and the social skills that you have mastered. As you become more competent in everyday relationships, you will find it easier to give up your addictions. Social competency means possessing positive abilities that allow you to interact with others in different situations, and in ways that are mutually beneficial, accepted and valued by society. Social competency is shared in intimate relationships where the individuals learn to value and reaffirm personal worth. In intimacy, this reciprocal message is given, "You are loved and cared for. You are respected and valued as I am."

Social skills are varied and many faceted because we humans are complex creatures. These skills are developmental in nature; two-year-olds have different levels of understanding and alternatives to choose from than ten-year-olds or adults do. As we progress in life, we continue to add new skills. Major transitions, such as being divorced, being widowed or moving to a new town, set the stage for learning new skills or reactivating old ones. The process of dealing with loss has the potential to deepen one's perspective as new understandings, attitudes and behaviors begin to surface. Social skills are tied to beliefs about ourselves based on family rules that were learned even before we began to talk. Belief systems and ways of coping become fairly set before the age of three. Rules on how to act are pieced and patched together out of the communication patterns and coping styles of the family. We automatically dust off the rule and use it until we decide it is time to learn new rules and skills.

Personal Goals For Releasing The Label Of Co-dependency

Which social skills do you need more practice on or have yet to learn? Check the areas in which you feel you need more information and training:

_____ Release old negative childhood scripts.

_____ Understand and own one's feelings.

_____ Take responsibility for personal actions.

_____ Express feelings and needs through "When you . . ., I feel" messages.

_____ Ask for what you want but be aware that you will not always get it.

_____ Say no when the situation calls for it without feeling guilty.

_____ Discriminate between taking the responsibility for another person and being responsible to that person.

_____ Allow others to take responsibility for their own actions.

_____ Recognize and respond appropriately to messages that are meant to provoke guilt.

_____ Use techniques of closure to bring about a decision on a topic.

_____ Recognize and correct self-destructive behavior.

_____ Replace negative thoughts about oneself with neutral or positive thoughts.

_____ Replace negative addictions with positive ones.

_____ Reject name-calling and blame tactics used by other people.

_____ Choose positive people for relationships.

_____ Give up the excessive need for approval.

_____ Accept compliments without discounting them.

_____ Stop the compulsion to please others.

_____ Take reasonable risks to expand and grow.

_____ Use daily affirmations to increase positive worth.

_____ View situations with humor and tolerance rather than getting off balance regarding small matters.

Dare To Speak Your Dreams

As you learn to move through your addictions and live in peace and harmony, more energy will become freed for creative endeavors. You will have more time and personal resources to accomplish your dreams. Mature individuals are in touch with their dreams of who they want to become and the goals they want to accomplish. Draw from a deep, deep level of your inner being as you ask yourself, "What do I really want?" Use the following affirmation to focus your energy on knowing and receiving what you truly desire (this is also a powerful affirmation to keep in your conscious mind when you are in a period of transition):

- I am willing to know what I want.
- I am willing to ask for it.
- I am willing to receive it when it comes.
- I am willing.
- I am.

Your Handprint Of Power

What personal goals do you have for your life? Write down the necessary ingredients that will make you happy in terms of finance, career, family, environment and relationships as well as your desire for peace and

harmony. _____

_____

_____

_____

_____

_____

You have within you many resources to draw from that will help you achieve these goals. Write down your positive qualities that have helped you survive up until now. What emotional, psychological and spiritual resources do you have? Take stock of your financial and material resources. Ask your

Higher Self to help you describe yourself accurately. _____

_____

_____

_____

_____

_____

_____

   Now put your hand on this paper where you have written your goals and dreams. Trace around your hand the way that you did when you were a kid. This is your handprint of power. Concentrate on the strength in your hands and your ability to commit to becoming a person of true integrity and trust. Know that you can make your goals and dreams come true if you are willing to make a commitment to doing what it takes to accomplish them.

   Commitment has power and destiny in it. Say to yourself, "This is my power. This is my peace. I can make these dreams come true. I put my handprint of power on my goals and dreams. I claim this power from myself." This personal power is your willingness to act in your best interests to obtain what you want. In working with your sense of personal power, you will gain new knowledge and learn new communication skills. You will make intelligent choices on your behalf and on behalf of those you love.

   Now hold one hand down on the page where you have written your goals and dreams, and place your other hand over your heart. Verbalize out loud what you have written. If you hear a part of yourself that feels you are not deserving, tell it that you speak from your yearning and your Highest Power, and tell it to go away. Speak your dreams loud and clear. Dare to speak your heart's desire out loud. Say them again and again, louder and louder until you feel the integration in your heart.

❧ NINE ❧

Balancing
The Emotions

When you can feel what you feel and say what you feel, you won't have to turn those bad feelings into body symptoms and pain.

Virginia Satir

Getting Off The Teeter-Totter Of Emotions.

One of the major functions in life is to learn to feel, accept and balance the emotions. As human beings, we are subject to feelings and emotional states. In co-dependency, the emotions swing back and forth from highs to lows. They are constantly out of balance as you overreact to daily events. Emotions are subjective reactions arising from the meaning we give to events that may give pleasure or pain. They come from our appraisal of events and our expectations as to what will happen. They are brought forth by situations that are important to our goals or concerns. Our abilities to handle an event successfully affect how we will feel about it. The predictability or the uncertainty of an event also helps determine our emotional reactions. Emotions prepare us to be ready to act.

It is natural for us to experience all the emotions with which we have been endowed. All emotions are okay and demand expression. All feelings, both those considered good and bad by society, are human. Our socialization and conditioning have taught us that some emotions should be considered positive, such as joy, happiness or excitement, because we feel good when they happen. Other emotions, such as depression, anger or jealousy, are to be considered negative because we experience discomfort and pain with them.

A more modern definition of positive and negative emotions is emerging from the current spirituality field. Emotions can be viewed in terms of how they affect the self-worth instead of viewing them in judgmental terms. Positive emotions are those that expand personal awareness and one's sense of well-being. Positive emotions are those that are expressed and released appropriately. Negative emotions, on the other hand, decrease or contract the individual and further poor self-esteem because of the way they are perceived and expressed. Negative emotions are merely feelings to which we need to add some peace.

A *Course In Miracles* tells us that there are two basic emotions of love and fear. Subconscious fear is underneath all of the emotions that we consider negative. There is generally a threat of loss behind any of the negative feelings. Anger is often a fear of threat to your physical body or to self-esteem. Jealousy is a fear that there isn't enough for you or that there will be a loss of the other person to someone else. Shame is a fear of being ridiculed. Depression is a fear that you are not worthy. Grief is the fear that the lost person will not return while attempting to keep that person close by through continual thoughts.

All emotions and behavior are purposeful, although at times it is hard to understand what purpose depression, anxiety, jealousy and anger may hold. Negative emotions are sometimes disguised as rational and logical reasons why you must limit yourself in some way. When you look beyond its painful aspect, each negative emotion has a gift for you. Our feelings are our teachers. One purpose of negative emotions is to invite you to look at that area in your life and learn to view it in a new way. It may continue to exist because it helps you in some way by protecting you from a subconscious threat. Fear may keep you safe by preventing you from taking risks. When the fear is faced and understood, it can be liberated. As Marilyn Ferguson said, "On the other side of fear is a freedom."

The left brain deals with linear, rational thinking. It is factual and judgmental, holding onto stressful emotional issues. Recent research suggests that negative emotions are processed in the right hemisphere of the brain. Negative issues can best be looked at by using an altered state of consciousness that involves right-brain processing. When something can be viewed differently using brain techniques, such as visual imagery or hypnosis, the negative emotional load can be lightened.

The right brain can perceive the total picture. It is creative, symbolic and nonjudgmental. It receives new information, which then can be used intuitively to see things differently and resolve the conflictual thinking. The technique of reframing is helpful in discharging emotions surrounding an event. Reframing is a technique described by Virginia Satir that allows you to perceive something in a new way by painting a new picture frame around it.

For example, loneliness is generally considered an undesirable, painful emotion. Viewed another way, loneliness is an emptiness that can be filled with whatever you choose to put in that space. Loneliness is a signal to give yourself a little bit more of whatever it is that you are lacking. Anger can be either positive or negative depending on the manner in which it is expressed. Anger expressed as a temper tantrum or as an attempt to control the actions of others is destructive to all concerned. However, anger that is acknowledged and spoken aloud in a nonblaming way to seek a solution to a common problem has positive effects. Depression indulged in resulting in self-pity and feelings of inertia can lead to deterioration. Depression that is expressed as part of the mourning process to let go of something of value that has been lost is also necessary as part of the healing process. Depression can be a signal that something in your life needs to be changed.

Learning to respect yourself more by honoring your range of emotions and expressing them appropriately is necessary in the process of recovery from co-dependency. You may have learned to numb your feeling in your need to survive in painful circumstances. Blocking of the emotions causes life's juices to dry up and the person stays in a nonliving state. How do you know if you are experiencing your feelings in an appropriate way? Listen to your language. If you are saying, "I think . . ." or "It seems to me as if . . .," along with giving long, rational arguments, then you are intellectualizing about a situation.

Emotions can be expressed on the body level as well as a feeling state. Listen to your body. Emotions have to go somewhere. They have to! If they are not expressed appropriately, they manifest on a physical level. If you are experiencing tightness, tension, conflict and have psychosomatic illnesses, then you have more to learn about better expressing what you feel. Experience your feelings to the fullest by opening yourself up to the learning behind the feelings. Instead of ignoring or suppressing your emotions, allow them their fullest range. Stay with them. Bring them to the forefront so that they will be released.

Make your feelings known first to yourself and then to others. Honor others by allowing them a safe place to express what they need to say without your becoming threatened. Learn to trust in the ability to be straight with each other and be vulnerable enough to say where you are and what is right for you. Develop friendships where it is safe for you to tell the truth about your feelings.

The Case Of The Lost Identity

What do you tell yourself to keep yourself all wrought up and upset all of the time? When you lie to yourself by refusing to express your emotions or by keeping yourself upset all of the time, you lose your identity. You can learn to monitor your thoughts and consciously choose which ones are helpful. Your thoughts, attitudes and belief systems can keep you off balance. Look at how these statements will keep you off balance: "I am justified in allowing _____ to do _____ and then get angry about it. I don't care what happens to me as long as _____ is taken care of." Imbalance means that you are slipping back into those old co-dependency thought patterns and attaching to the negative emotions.

The balancing of emotions is a minute-by-minute choice that you can learn to make. Look for the threat to your physical self or your self-esteem behind the negative statements. State your feelings more openly using the "When you . . ., I feel . . ." message. When faced with imbalance, find your tilt point where you start to lose your center of gravity. Bring yourself back to balance by deep breathing. Listen to what you know instead of what you fear.

The choice lies with accepting personal responsibility to perceive situations in new ways. How you express yourself in a given situation may be nothing more than a lifelong habit. You may be so used to the automatic habit that you do not even recognize it when you do it. The first step to unlearning a habit is to bring it to a conscious level where it can be examined. Through learning to notice the painful emotions as they surface, you can analyze and restructure them. Feeling the emotion and recognizing it is the first step; this takes you past the numbing coping mechanism.

You cannot directly control your emotions by sheer acts of will. Trying to control anger, depression or jealousy simply puts more energy into it. Yet you can learn to reframe those emotions that cause pain, and influence them by changing your belief systems, attitudes, language and behavior. You can take responsibility for what you tell yourself about the events in your life. The dysfunctional ways of reacting to a situation, such as blaming, denying, distracting, intellectualizing or placating, avoid personal responsibility. Modern day therapies repeat what the ancient philosophers taught. No one can make you feel a certain way. Events do happen to you without your being able to control them. What you can learn to control is how you perceive and react to events. As the old saying goes, "You can't keep misery from coming around, but you don't have to give it a chair to sit on."

Choosing To Feel Good

Catch yourself in the act when you start to express an emotion that causes tension in your body. Monitor your thoughts that have elements of worry, doubt, anger, depression and guilt in them. Determine where you place the responsibility for these emotions. No one can **make** you feel anything. Your feelings are your personal prerogative. Erasmus said, "No one is injured save by himself." Ask yourself what you are telling yourself to become so upset. Listen to the language of your thinking for statements that project blame on someone else.

- My friend depresses me when . . .
- My dad makes me feel bad when . . .
- She makes me mad when . . .
- My mother makes me feel guilty when . . .
- You make me happy when . . .

Write down the typical statement you use to project the blame for your internal emotions on someone else.

_____

_____

_____

Now make the choice of taking responsibility for your own feelings. Instead of saying a "He, she, they make me feel . . ." statement, change the beginning of the sentence to one of personal responsibility.

Change the pronoun to the first person. I make myself feel _____

_____ when _____.

Choice about how to feel about a situation, no matter how adverse the circumstances, is the ultimate freedom. The next step is to recognize the role of personal choice in the internal statement that you are making. Change the sentence again emphasizing how you are letting external events influence your emotional state.

I choose to feel _____

when _____.

Remember, it is not helpful to justify your behavior or your past behavior. If you find yourself justifying your unhappy emotions, say to yourself, "Do I want to be right or have peace of mind?" If you need to explain yourself to others or even to yourself over and over, know that you are hooking yourself back into a choice to feel bad.

Now, honor the emotion that comes forth. Allow its full expression so that you can learn from it. Your feeling is your teacher. Just say to yourself, lovingly and gently, "Oh yes, there are those feelings of guilt, hate and jealousy coming up again to teach me. There must be a message for me in this incident." Determine if this emotion is in your best interest at present. Is it contributing to your personal growth or is it an old habit surfac-

ing to be examined? _____

_____

What is the physical or emotional threat behind the emotion? _____

_____

Is this a real threat or an irrational one based on an old survival rule? _____

_____

As you learn more about yourself, you will find that you are reacting less emotionally to things that used to bother you greatly. Finding your inner peace and harmony in daily activities is a sign that you are making progress. Use the formula of "When you . . ., I feel . . ." to define your overcharged feelings. Write down the emotional overreactions that you have experienced recently that are still unresolved.

_____

_____

_____

_____

_____

Which emotions still need to be brought into more balance? _____

_____

_____

With this knowledge, write down specific personal goals that will bring you

to a place of peace and harmony. _____

_____

_____

_____

_____

_____

The decision to feel good must be made again and again. This affirmative decision of recognizing that you have a choice will help you change those typically painful emotions of a milder nature. When you find yourself becoming angry, confused or depressed, do not blame yourself. Adding self anger and criticism to an already negative state locks you into it even more.

Look around for balanced individuals whom you can use as role models until you develop those qualities that they project and become your own role model. Be in touch daily with the lessons that you are facing and the aspects of your personality that you are changing. Remember, change does not occur when you become other than who you are, but instead when you become more of who you are.

Learned Helplessness And Co-dependency

Two of the more challenging emotions to bring into balance are sadness and depression. People caught in co-dependency often suffer from reactive depression. Reactive depression is different from ongoing organic depression, which is a result of a faulty biochemical makeup that may have a genetic basis. Reactive depression is a belief in one's own helplessness that is triggered by a specific circumstance. People react to a loss that they have suffered, such as a death of a loved one, or a relationship over which they have no control. The loss can be a psychological one such as feelings of being devalued by someone. Depression is often anger turned inward that is experienced as worthlessness and self-blame. Helplessness and the accompanying depression and loss of self-esteem can be a major component in co-dependent behavior.

The depression that is often experienced in an unhappy relationship is a reaction to the loss of the dream of finding happiness in the relationship. Staying in a relationship that is emotionally unhealthy is a common cause of depression. Depression develops as a signal from the body that the lifestyle is very wrong for the individual. Often when changes are made to better the situation, the depression goes away.

The research literature is exploring psychological trauma victims and linking their behavior with the theory of learned helplessness. Learned helplessness is a concept that is documented by the researcher Martin Seligman and his colleagues. In learned helplessness, individuals find that their actions do not make a difference in what happens to them. The symptoms are passivity, lack of assertiveness, a general slowdown in responding and depression. Individuals are repeatedly exposed to a situation beyond their control so they become passive and feel paralyzed. They have learned that no matter what they do, it does not make a difference. Nothing these individuals do seems to work so they give up and become immobile. When escape is possible, they can become so paralyzed that they cannot leave the bad situation. Seligman theorizes that people's feedback mechanisms can become altered to the point where the ability to learn new ways of acting is disrupted. People cannot make a difference in their world so they stop trying. Learned helplessness can become an underlying factor in depression and has been attributed as the reason why some women tend to remain in unhealthy, dependent relationships.

Learned helplessness can be specific to one situation, such as not doing well in math, or it can spill over into many areas of life in a generalized way where the person typically is a victim. Passivity can become a coping mechanism with the "poor me" victim mentality and heavy placator behavior that serves to deal with stress. Placators believe that they will experience less grief and pain if they accept their fate of submissively giving in to others. This is a false assumption because the research documents that nonassertive people are taken for granted. Acting in a submissive manner sets up the occasion for mental and physical abuse to occur. People with extreme learned helplessness develop a pathological tolerance for degradation and intimidation from others.

Seligman's concept of stress inoculation states that individuals should be taught a wide repertoire of coping responses and provided with small failures so that they learn to overcome adversity through their own problem solving. Success in problem solving in the face of failure seems to be the primary factor that distinguishes mastery-oriented people from learned helplessness people. Mastery-oriented people use positive self-statements to help them respond to life's stresses and traumas. They learn to rely on their own internal resources to solve their problems. They develop internal statements that are very task-oriented to keep them focused on completing the task. They provide their own internal cheering section to obtain mastery when they are faced with failure. They show a high commitment to finishing tasks that are important to them and place emphasis on their personal effort in success. In doing so they feel a sense of control over the environment, which is related to a strong inner sense of self-esteem.

In addition, Seligman's research suggests that the "explanatory style" or ways that individuals explain what happens to them contribute to events in their life. People with pessimistic explanatory styles have greater problems in relationships and in health resulting in lowered immune function. The internal self-statements about performance are the underlying factors in whether a person becomes helpless or not. What you expect is what you get! Learned helpless people tell themselves, "I'm no good. I never could do . . . This is hard. I'd like to go do . . . instead." Mastery-oriented people have a different internal set of statements. They say, "Oh boy, this is a challenge. I'll try it this way to see if I can get it. This is fun. There now, I'm on track." With their mind-set of hope and positive expectations, they perceive success and actually achieve it!

Determining Your Patterns Of Helplessness And Mastery

Look at how your beliefs about yourself and your self-statements affect your performance in different situations. You have natural abilities and talents in some areas that are easy for you. Other tasks are more difficult. The best way to succeed at the more difficult tasks is to approach them with a positive mind-set and not fall back into those old tapes of how helpless you are.

In what areas of your life do you have appropriate coping strategies?

_____

_____

In what areas do you fall apart, use statements of blame and anger, and display helplessness? _____

_____

What do you tell yourself when you feel helpless? If you are not aware of your self-statements, attempt a difficult task, talk it through out loud and write down what you say. _____

_____

_____

When you are excited and challenged by a difficult task, what do you say to yourself to keep you going? _____

Pogo was right when he said, "We have met the enemy and they is us!" Be aware of how you play your own worst enemy and cheerleader during task completion. What critical statements that cause you to dissolve into

helplessness do you want to release? _____

When you hear yourself making those internal negative statements about how dumb, stupid and worthless you are, be aware that you have taken on someone else's critical message about yourself. Your language defines who you are. Use words that define you in a positive manner. Make the decision to substitute mastery-oriented statements such as, "Yes, this is hard, but it's worth the effort," "I haven't learned this **yet**!" "I'll keep working and I'll get it . . .," or "Deep breathing will calm me down so I can figure this out."

Learned helplessness starts in childhood. Behavior similar to that of post-traumatic stress disorder seen in veterans of war has been found in children of extremely dysfunctional homes. Children are traumatized when they are unable to affect the outcome of events of their unpredictable parents and face life events they cannot control. Initially children protest what they cannot control by becoming angry, verbally hostile or acting out. Later the numbing state of withdrawal and isolation results, and children become adept at shutting off those emotions that are unpleasant.

Common themes found in the learned helplessness of children from dysfunctional families include a lack of perceived control or mastery of the situation, poor coping techniques, and social isolation and avoidance of social support. Children spend valuable time worrying, acting out or feeling frightened in response to confused family role identities, fear of parental violence, or the atmosphere of stress and tension that surrounds the dysfunctional behavior of the parents. Contact with others is avoided as children may be embarrassed by the behavior of their parents and avoid bringing their friends home in order to keep the family secrets. They may cut off the necessary social support that might normalize and buffer them from the problems in their family.

To develop maturity and trust, children need to learn that their wants can be satisfied by their asking for them to be met in a world that is safe. Learning to trust both themselves and others is one of the major tasks of life. Children need to learn that they can make an impact on their environment in a positive, consistent and predictable way. Patterns of personal power and predictability can be learned at a later age in life if they have not been learned during the early years.

Current researchers are studying the coping styles of healthy adolescents who come out of severely dysfunctional families. Appropriate techniques to deal with stress separated the young people who functioned well from those who did not, in later life. Those who did well were aware of their parents' illness but concluded that they did not cause it. They found their own identity that was separate from the family, which allowed them to separate psychologically from their parents. They developed close relationships and built a good social support system. They learned problem-solving skills and developed coping styles that helped them feel some control over what happened to them.

They became committed to projects that were personally satisfying. They used techniques of relaxation and incorporated exercise into their routine as a means of stress management. Some left the home to live with relatives or friends; others assumed the caretaking role of younger brothers and sisters, and tried to get help for their parents. The positive coping strategies helped provide the healthy adolescents with internal strength to make the best out of a bad situation.

Releasing Anger Turned Inward

One of the biggest challenges for Doormats is to learn to balance the emotion of anger and express it in an appropriate way. Co-dependent people often have a lot of anger but often have strong should-not messages about acknowledging or expressing it. They have been brought up with heavy messages of being a "good little girl or boy," which means never showing displeasure over anything. The stuffing of anger over a period of years results in numbness, unresolved conflict and psychosomatic illnesses. Anger may masquerade as depression because tears can be a cover for anger. Recent research has shown that repression of strong emotions and personal needs may lead to a type of personality that is prone to cancer. Other research has linked anger and hostility with the Type-A personality that is prone to heart attacks. If you find yourself continually becoming angry, then be aware that you have some important learning to do in this area. Anger has a purpose in our lives. It can energize you and can help you change things. Anger can have a burning power that helps cut through a negative experience like a sword. Thus, anger does have its value.

The base of anger is fear. It is that primitive reflex where the person goes into the fight or flight pattern. For it to occur, the person must perceive that a transgression occurred, and there is a fear of loss of some kind. For anger to occur, the person must take the infringement seriously. The situation must be seen as negative. The threat can either be a direct or an unintentional act of another person. It can be a physical threat with violence to our self, territory or possessions. It can also be psychological where our sense of self-esteem feels threatened or our expectations are thwarted. Anger surfaces when we view that the rules and standards of our society are being violated. The degree or proportion of anger depends on how we perceive the seeming unreasonableness, arbitrariness or impropriety of the offense.

Stating The Necessary And Sorting Out The Unnecessary Anger

Here is an exercise that helps you sort out the positive and harmful aspects of anger. Record these statements on a tape player in a slow, dreamy speed using a soothing voice. As you listen to your tape, place yourself in a meditative state to gain full understanding of these important lessons on anger. Let your unconscious mind work through the anger issues that come up as you listen to the tape.

I place myself in a calm relaxed state of mind to gain information about myself. Angry thoughts about my condition often cross my mind. I am angry at myself for having produced such a situation. I am angry at my family for not understanding my needs. I am angry at . . . for not giving me the support I need. There is a part of me that does not want to be that "good little girl or boy." That is understandable. I am human, and anger is one emotion that humans have. It's very natural for me to have these emotions.

I begin to understand the purpose of anger in my life. Some anger is appropriate and honest; some is self-destructive. I recognize that there is anger within me, either expressed through my thoughts internally or verbally toward others. When the demands of my life exceed my personal resources and I feel a threat, I become angry. I am aware of how unnecessary anger has affected my peace of mind and mental health. The anger has caused a strain on my physical health.

I sort out the source of my anger — what I can change and what I cannot. I come to a better understanding and acceptance of the purpose of anger in my life. I take all the time I need to work through my anger. I give myself permission to feel anger in situations that are unjust. I understand I need not give up my anger at any situation until it is right for me to do so.

I am willing to outgrow what no longer fits me. I seek an end to the unreasonable, self-defeating part of anger. I stop criticizing myself for being angry and put my energy into understanding and resolving it. I am gentle and loving with myself as I gain new insights into how best to express my anger. I refuse to be a victim of painful, unproductive thoughts that continually cross my mind. I do not attach to unnecessary grudges and resentments.

I seek new insights into how I can express myself more fully so that I need not build up anger. I find ways to assert myself appropriately by saying what is right for me. I express legitimate anger in meaningful ways. I make my needs known to others. I use the "When you . . ., I feel . . ." formula over and over.

When unnecessary anger crowds my mind, I let the feelings go on past. I become more mellow and do not allow little things to upset me as much. I am less irritable and more forgiving of the limitations of others. I am less critical and more forgiving of the limitations of myself and more accepting of my own mistakes and shortcomings. When something upsets me, I speak calmly and quietly stating what I need. When I feel frustration, I find ways to express myself immediately in an appropriate manner. When something is important to me, I am forceful, firm and tactful in letting others know how I feel.

I channel my anger into areas I can change to make things better for me. When I am upset by what others have done, I try to understand the motivation behind their actions. I question my assumption that their reason is to deliberately cause me harm. When others are angry with me, I look for the threat to the other people's self-esteem and how their expectation of me has not been met. I analyze whether my own experiences in the past color my angry reactions of today. I become more aware of how today's anger reflects an unresolved irritation from my past. I analyze the underlying "I should/ should not" or "they should/should not" messages behind my anger.

I see how actions of others that upset me are merely reflections of those parts of myself with which I am uncomfortable. I am aware of how my choice to be helpless in a situation sets me up for later anger. I release myself from irrational, unwelcome resentment by stating my feelings openly.

I welcome the calm and peace that this release allows me. I have the right to understand and accept all parts of me, even my negative emotions. I choose to live a calm, tranquil life free from unnecessary anger. I am me: secure, peaceful and serene. Peace takes over and becomes the center of my life. I turn inward now and listen to my own Inner Wisdom as I continue to work through my unresolved, irrational anger.

TEN

Going Through
The Tight Passage

Set the ever present, intrusive ego aside.

Zen Proverb

The Not So Lovely Parts Of Ourselves

Jungian theory states that many subpersonalities make up our total being. They are all partial aspects of the character. Within the ego is the *Part Who Needs To Be Taken Care Of* and the *Part That Is Not Dependent On Others*. There is the *Domineering Part* and the *Submissive Part*. There is the *Courageous Part* and the *Frightened Part*, etc. Within is the Blamer who is the critical judge and the Placator who plays the role of the guilty offender. We also have the Distractor Part who seeks diversions from the conflict and the Super-Reasonable Part who is totally above all that is going on using tactics of denial. Also present is the Highest Self, which expresses the yearning and the drive toward wholeness and integration.

These parts have split off from the total personality at times of traumatic events in those early years. Pain and the accompanying feelings of betrayal

133

and shame have caused fragments of the self to develop and remain buried in the subconscious mind. These little selves are purposeful and helpful in some way. Often they help deal with some type of threat. Each part rises in turn out of fear for the defense of the individual to keep things at status quo and avoid chaos.

Living in a society that says certain personality traits are wrong, causes individuals to try to deny and repress the negative aspects of their personality because of deep-seated feelings of embarrassment and inadequacy. This is the Jungian concept of the Shadow Self: those dark, negative parts of the ego that we are uncomfortable with. Yet, however hard we try to repress these dark parts, they rise and come to the surface time and time again.

Jung believed that the way individuals try to resolve their deep underlying conflict is by experiencing the life situations that bring them into focus. He wrote, "The psychological rule is that when an inner situation is not made conscious, it happens outside, as fate. That is to say, when the individual remains undivided and does not become conscious of his inner contradictions, the world must perforce act out the conflict and be torn into opposite halves."

Recovery from co-dependency is ongoing. Life presents you with a continual meeting of yourself time and again in different situations. What you do not deal with well is presented to you in different guises of conflictual situations so that you have the opportunity to work it out. One way to look at the complex pattern of your life is to examine the patterns and themes that repeat themselves. The phrase "My own comes to me," expresses this sentiment. Your "own" can be the same type of petty tyrant, the same issue coming back around, the same frustrations or conflict, or the same negative beliefs that you hold. The old Scottish proverb acknowledges this age-old wisdom: "What's for ye, comes to ye." The positive things in terms of positive relationships and abundance that you experience are also your "own." You draw to you what you manifest in your unconscious mind. It is the spiritual journey that is leading you home. Going home is a metaphor for finding your True Self.

The process of going home is never easy. It is rife with fear, risk taking and adjustment to continual change. We may go kicking and screaming along the path but all the same, the way is there for us. It takes us deeper and deeper into ourselves until we strip away that which is unnecessary. The process teaches us to build a clearer, simpler, more harmonious existence. It is a surrender experience as we let go of control and the dark parts of the ego. Trust the process. Trust the journey that proceeds onward to bring you home to yourself.

Identifying What Is Your Own

Take an inventory of the beautiful relationships, career successes and material possessions that you have brought into your life. See what you have manifested through believing in yourself in specific areas and working hard to achieve your goals. Write your version of "My own comes to me."

_____

_____

_____

_____

_____

Now look at the areas of your life where you typically feel negative emotions. What experiences do you have that bring about denial, guilt, confusion, depression or anxiety? These too are your own. There is a message for you beneath the underlying emotion. This is your homework list. Write the unresolved issues in your life that you have been trying to work through since childhood.

_____

_____

_____

_____

_____

Maturity and harmony in life are the result of these parts being integrated into the total personality by acknowledging the darkness of the Shadow Self and bringing it to the light. There must be a confrontation of the _Self That Is Feared_ to find the _Self That Really Is_. Integration comes by learning to accept the disowned parts. This happens when the individual learns to love those not so lovely parts through acceptance. Acceptance of the fragmented part, and the accompanying negative emotions and self-forgiveness for not being perfect, is the key to release of the Shadow Subpersonalities. A situation of complete trust and safety helps the individual face the Shadow Self. The dark parts can hold the greatest gifts for you as they hold the keys to release you from lifelong fear and shame.

Jung used the metaphor of the shadow as a tight passage that must be traveled to come through on the other side. The only way to get there was

Who Am I?

Paul, The People Pleaser

Self-Limiting Louis

Self-Blame Sam

Big Bad Boris

by giving up the concept of duality and by, in his words, "letting in the darkness." He wrote, ". . . the shadow is a tight passage, a narrow door, whose painful constriction no one is spared who goes down to the deep well. But one must learn to know oneself in order to know who one is. For what comes after the door is, surprisingly enough, a boundless expanse full of unprecedented uncertainty, with apparently no inside and no outside, no above and no below, no here and no there, no mine and no thine, and no good and no bad. It is where the realm of the sympathetic system, the soul of everything living begins; where I am indivisibly this and that; where I experience the other in myself and the other-than-myself experiences me."

Integrating The Shadow Self

This process is based on Virginia Satir's Transformational Process and the theories of Carl Jung. Center yourself by breathing deeply. Go to your loving inspired place of Inner Wisdom. Put yourself in a state of deep relaxation and allow the steps of this integration process to happen. The *Steps of Creativity* are included as headings to show how your subconscious mind can work through problems on its own when you give it permission.

Preparation

Gather data on a concern that you are facing in your life. What is an issue

that is currently bothering you? _____

_____

Incubation

Turn the problem over to your subconscious mind. What is the feeling

behind the concern? _____

_____

What is your feeling about your feeling? _____

_____

Where do you feel the feeling in your body? _____

_____

What negative quality in yourself are you in touch with (greed, lust, shame, hatred, guilt, jealousy, etc.)? _____

_____

This is a part of your Shadow Self.
What is the longing regarding the feeling? What do you want to have happen with this feeling? _____

_____

Visualize the feeling. Turn it into an image or metaphor. _____

_____

Add movement to the metaphor and allow the subconscious mind to give you information about the meaning of the metaphor.

Illumination

Draw from your subconscious mind whatever you need to help understand and accept the Shadow Part. What purpose does it have in your life? _____

Greed, for example, is necessary to help you survive so that you won't give away all of your possessions. Anger might be used to express your bottom line beyond which you do not allow people to trespass.

How has this part of your Shadow Self kept you safe? _____

_____

From what does it protect you? _____

_____

What is the opposite quality that counterbalances the Shadow Part? _____

_____

See how the positive and negative qualities work together. For example, greed and generosity operate in tandem to give you balance. Although the two qualities are at opposing ends of the continuum, they can be considered one and the same.

Have the two qualities talk to each other and work out ways to work together in balance. Neither needs to be threatened by the other.

Validation

Validate your Shadow Part by bringing it into the light. See the negative part of yourself being bathed in light. Have it feel the warmth and loving. Tell it that you do not need to resist it anymore but only desire to understand its purpose in your life. _____

_____

Tell it that you know it is not entirely who you are but just a part of who you are. _____

_____

Tell it that you will stop trying to squelch it and control it. _____

_____

Remind yourself that you no longer need to criticize yourself whenever you start to feel bad about this negative quality. Tell it you will be gentle and loving with it when it comes up again in this concern or in a new issue.

_____

Reassure it that the opposite quality is there to give balance and that you will never allow it to run away with your life. _____

_____

Now, from your Higher Power, focus your most loving energy on that negative aspect of your personality. Tell it that you love it and do not need to deny it. Ask it what it needs to feel more comfortable. _____

_____

How can you act differently now that you have this knowledge? _____

_____

Reach out and embrace that part of the Shadow which has previously been of concern to you. As Jung said, "When we face what we fear, the desert starts to bloom."

The Surrender Experience

The process of surrender is an integral part of recovery from co-dependency as well as any other addictive behavior. Because of our cultural heritage, the surrender experience is a challenge to understand. The beliefs that we have grown up with in western society give continual messages about acquiring and attaching to the things of the world. Success is defined as obtaining and holding onto power and material possessions. We are told that we have the right to feel good and to go for all that we can get. Yet within these messages lie the roots of addictions. Jung's theory of individuation, where the conflict between the various aspects of the Total Self are accepted and integrated, describes how surrender liberates the individual. Buddhist psychology also describes this process of surrender which is similar to the process of letting go in 12-step programs.

The Total Self consists of the ego mind and the God Self. According to Jungian theory, there is a split between these two parts of the personality early in life. The depth of the chasm between the two selves is a result of how early and how violently the split took place. The process of individuation allows you to learn to exist as a whole, undivided human being. This is the spiritual journey that is embarked on as we move through the various developmental tasks and stages of life, beginning at birth and continuing through death. Jung wrote, "This is an ultimately religious process which requires a correspondingly religious attitude where the ego's will gives in to God's will."

The ego mind is the center of the conscious personality that chooses and attaches to objects, activities, people and belief systems to meet its own self-seeking ambitions and unresolved power needs. It is the little self or lower self that is necessary for everyday living. The ego lives in the world of illusion as it does not see the total picture. It contains those Shadow Parts of the personality that attach and cling because all they know is fear. It tries to find happiness by attaching to things of the world. For short periods of time it finds a narcissistic type of joy in possessions or activities. Being defined by the messages of our materialistic society, it is limited by beliefs of incompleteness and selfishness. Addictions are a universal experience and product of our civilized society as they arise from the incomplete ego mind. When you find yourself caught in constant strife and melodrama reacting to daily events, you are operating from the ego.

Without the ego we would not survive. It is needed to ensure that the physical needs of the body will be met so that we can live. The ego mind is rigid and stays asleep, building the wall of denial around itself as the strong need to survive precludes its knowing about the God Self. The ego projects its power outward turning it over to an external source. It chooses substances, activities or a person to find comfort and meaning, and to define who it is. It continually brings us back to those addictions until we work through them. In order to protect its very existence, the ego tries to prevent painful material from arising from the subconscious. It uses the obsessive thinking and craving about addictions to block new information from coming forth so that threatening thoughts are repressed. The individual uses the addiction as a misguided attempt to heal itself. Addictions thus become the tools for survival of the ego. They stem from the belief of "I am not enough. I am not complete. I must have . . . to feel good." Fear, threat and separation are the underlying mechanisms of the Ego Self. The ego is transcended only when unmet needs are worked through. Denial of the ego needs only keeps the individuals where they are.

The Total Self is conceptualized as containing both the ego mind and the God Self. The God Self is whole, complete and knows the connection among all living things. The God Self knows unconditional love. In its completion, it accepts the limitations, imperfections and partial nature of the ego. Within the God Self lies the Observer Self. That is the part that detaches from the overemotionality of the ego, and steps back and watches what is going on. The Observer cautions you to act instead of reacting and helps you make choices through impartiality and reason. If the God Self is healthy and alive in the individual, it can function to bring creativity in to break down the ego. Suffering can become the impetus to break into the hold that the ego has on the individual.

Individuation occurs when the ego mind becomes aligned with the God Self. The dark parts of the Shadow have been worked through, and peace and harmony prevail. Addictions are accepted and understood for what they are as attaching undue meaning to something that exists in the external world. The Buddha was right when he said that life is made of suffering which results from attachment to the things of this world. Giving up the attachment to the addictive meaning of a substance, activity or person shifts the individual to a higher level of consciousness. Individuation means finding the true source of happiness within one's self. It is to find meaning within one's own being.

There appears to be a critical point related to hitting bottom on a given issue that must be experienced if vast changes are to occur. Ego death and the eventual rebirth and integration of the personality happen only when the pain is severe enough to overcome the ego defenses. In a physical or spiritual crisis the brink can be approached and faced so that the superinflated ego can be transcended. This critical point may be related to a life-threatening illness, a significant loss or the passage of an important developmental milestone such as the 40th birthday. A crisis can be the signal for change by pounding home the knowledge that the old way no longer works. Suffering can be the prelude to the main theme of transformation.

The Law of Dissipated Structure says that things must fall apart in order for them to be restructured. The importance of this law was recently recognized in the scientific community with the Nobel Peace Prize being awarded to its author, Ilya Prigogine. The law states that in order for things to come together in a new way, the old must be dissolved. This law also applies to human beings. When threatened with a critical point, the ego clutches harder trying to preserve its very existence. The **no** has to be screamed long and loud enough to come to the final **yes!** The surrender does not diminish individuals. Paradoxically, the surrender experience opens up people and puts them in touch with their personal power, which is the willingness and ability to act in their own best interest. The old system gives way to the new if the fear is pushed through. If the fear is not faced, the individual retreats to the old destructive patterns again.

The journey beyond the ego is the journey of the heart and is a process of spiritual emergence. This vivid process helps break into the meaning given to the attachments and addictions of the Ego Self. It is the attachment to the meaning that is given to the substance, activity or person that must be addressed. The process of transformation includes the recognition and acknowledgment of one's responsibility in contributing to a problem, despair over the powerlessness of the situation and turning the situation over to a Higher Power. It is that quantum leap between the despair of "My God, my God, why hast Thou forsaken me?" and the acceptance of "Thy will be done."

What is surrendered are the negative parts of the ego that are embraced and accepted. The surrender is to the God Self. The death of the partial selves of the ego includes going deep into a state of humility and helplessness, and feeling the yearning to be whole while asking for release. Forgiveness at a deep level is accomplished through humility and a longing to be free. With the release comes gratitude and celebration. This is the rebirth as the individual expands to a higher level of consciousness. The process is a giving up of a significant portion of the ego that results in a personality change as the individual's belief systems are dramatically altered. Strength and integrity are felt as the integration of the personality is accomplished. A deep sense of gratitude and humility accompanies this surrender experience. Albert Camus described this death/rebirth experience when he said, "In the midst of winter, I finally learned that there was in me an invincible summer."

Moving through these experiences has been described as a "paradox of intense effort that only becomes effective through total surrender, the unlikely marriage of trying with not trying," by George Leonard in *The Silent*

Pulse. The process of focused surrender begins with an issue that the Higher Self brings forth to resolve. Time and mental energy is spent on this issue as it takes on monumental importance in the person's life. He focuses deeply on the issue and mulls it over and over. He looks at it in the same old way, recycling old beliefs, feelings and behaviors, and experiences great pain and confusion. The mind tries to force the issue through great determination and, in doing so, personal energy is depleted. When the individual reaches the point of total exhaustion, resignation and despair, his ego is relinquished. He says, "I give up," and admits helplessness and hopelessness, turning the issue over to his Higher Power. Then the transformation occurs with tears, intense emotion and feelings of relief. The intense focus has helped the individual to view the issue in a new way to reframe and restructure it.

Determining Your Holy And Unholy Needs

In recovery from co-dependency, the unhealthy meanings to the dysfunctional love relationship are surrendered. Dependency on another human being at the expense of one's self is released. The old unhealthy needs based on the desperation to be whole by merging with or rescuing another person can be dropped, one by one.

Take inventory now of where you are in regard to your needs. View your needs as specific addictions that stand between you and wholeness. Follow your sense of what needs to be corrected as you mark this checklist of unholy needs:

_____ An addiction to taking care of someone else
_____ An addiction to thinking obsessively about someone else
_____ An addiction to rescuing and changing another person
_____ An addiction to being the teacher or the expert
_____ An addiction to sex
_____ An addiction to possessing someone else
_____ An addiction to carrying the burdens of someone else
_____ An addiction to controlling someone else
_____ An addiction to being perfect
_____ An addiction to suffering
_____ An addiction to the excitement of the ups and downs of crisis
_____ An addiction to using someone else to provide energy and excitement
_____ An addiction to being immobilized in a relationship
_____ An addiction to idolizing and worshipping another person
_____ An addiction to feeling special and important because of another person's interest in you
_____ An addiction to having "romance" in your life

Needs change as you grow and mature. Holy needs are ones that contribute to your wholeness and come out of the longing to be free from dependency. Unholy needs are those that are obsessive and destructive in nature, taking you away from your true spiritual self. Unholy needs are merely illusions coming out of your beliefs of being unworthy. You can give up the attachments to the meanings that you have assigned them.

It comes down to what you believe about yourself and where you choose to put your energy. Examine your unholy needs and change them to preferences. Make the choice to be in relationships that are not obsessive in nature. Use this second checklist to get in touch with your holy needs. This list can also be used for daily affirmations.

_____ I choose to have recognition from within and no longer look outside myself for equality.
_____ I choose to feel whole and complete.
_____ I choose to be happy in and by myself first, and then in my relationship.
_____ I choose to be a separate individual not dependent on another person for my happiness.
_____ I choose freedom over the need to control.
_____ I choose to have a balanced relationship with myself and others.
_____ I choose to be my most loving True Self.

The 12-Step programs successfully bring the person to that critical point where the old can fall away to bring order out of the chaos created by the addictive behavior. They offer an acknowledgment and surrender formula that can be applied to many different problems in life: I am powerless over . . ., only a Power greater than myself can remove this problem. Carl Jung was influential in helping develop the underlying philosophy in Alcoholics Anonymous. He wrote to the founder Bill W. that addictions are a quest for spiritual seeking and treatment required a spiritual approach rather than a psychological one.

Most religious traditions have a concept of spiritual healing and of giving one's self over to a greater consciousness than one's self. The surrender process is similar in nature to the life-altering experiences regarding death/ rebirth described by the mystics in the spiritual literature down through the ages. The Buddha said that life contained suffering and that release from suffering could only be achieved by giving up attachment. The Upanishads and the Tao both describe the value in nonattachment to the things of the world. Jesus underwent the surrender experience on the cross and was resurrected. His act of surrender is described by the Gospel of St. Mark, "Abba, Father all things are possible unto thee; take away this cup from me; nevertheless not what I will, but what thou wilt." St. John of the Cross wrote of the Dark Night of the Soul where the depths must be descended so that transformation could occur.

Surrender, forgiveness and gratitude are the elements of the healing process. You may have had such an experience where your belief systems were radically changed. Immature expectations and attachments to the idea of a substance, activity or person are relinquished in this surrender process. The surrender process changes your meanings of things. The Sufi proverb expresses this well, "Words have to die if humans are to live."

The old belief, "I am nothing without the addiction," is transformed by the spiritual side of one's nature through a breakthrough in consciousness.

The ego's attachment to the fear is broken as the process of death/rebirth moves individuals out of fear consciousness into love. Individuals forgive themselves, 'others or God. Gratitude is expressed to the Higher Power for the profound changes that take place. The following statements that describe the process from co-dependent addiction to release show the shift from a fear mentality to a consciousness that is love:

1. The belief that "I do not have a problem with _____" is denial based on illusion originating in the ego.
2. The self-statement of "I should stop _____" comes from the fear and guilt of the ego.
3. The knowing of "I am helpless over _____" is the way the God Self allows the hitting bottom to restructure the faulty belief system.
4. The decision of "I want to stop _____" is based on the yearning perpetuated by the God Self.
5. The receptivity of stating, "I surrender my resistance to _____ and turn the problem over to a Higher Power" demonstrates a manifestation of trust and faith.
6. The resolution of "I will stop _____" originates in the God Self bringing forth inner determination and strength.
7. The living of the "I am a beautiful whole person without the addictive need of _____" is based on loving of one's self. This final step happens as the different parts of the personality are integrated.

At a recent conference on world religions, three prerequisites were determined to be necessary for spiritual evolution. Humility, gratitude and humor were the necessary ingredients for growth. The surrender experience provides humility and gratitude. Humor about one's situation in life can also come with a different type of surrender.

The Cosmic Joke is that nothing is so serious that it can't be viewed from a situation of humor. When you really understand the Cosmic Joke, you may laugh hysterically as you begin to see the ridiculousness of co-dependent behavior; this is the Cosmic Giggle!

Once you "get" the Cosmic Joke, the world is viewed as a brighter place and everything is perceived in a different perspective. It is hard to take yourself seriously. You can laugh about your tragic past because you no longer have to relive it. This expanded perception helps you move through self-limiting beliefs and fears. You feel lighter as the burden of seeing things negatively has been removed. Thomas Heywood was correct when he said, "The World's a theater, the earth a stage, which God and Nature do with actors fill." The Cosmic Joke helps us know that we are all players in the great drama we call life. Nothing happens by accident. The soap opera that we participate in is all divine order. We do have to choose roles. The choice is to choose roles in which we can have fun, laugh and play. The paradox is that it is hard to take it all seriously and yet we can't fail to take it seriously.

The understanding of the Cosmic Joke may be there on an intellectual level yet that is not the true understanding. The real understanding comes when the journey is made from the head to the heart. This happens only when this knowledge comes from a "gut" level instead of a "head" level. Jesus, the Buddha and other great spiritual teachers had this knowing of the "rightness" of things and expressed it in their delightful childlike natures.

All Things Are Resolved In Love

Because forgiveness and surrender are important to accomplish on the way to recovery, here is a second exercise using affirmations to assist your process. Copy these statements and place in a prominent place, such as the bathroom mirror or the kitchen sink, where they will catch your eye so that you can repeat them several times a day. Place your hands gently on your throat to make an X as you repeat the following affirmations. Close your eyes and feel the wisdom of releasing all that you have been caught up with for a long, long time and now no longer need.

- I accept myself for who I am.
- I do this loving release exercise to promote my growth.
- I view each conflictual situation as an opportunity for promoting positive change.
- I see my painful feelings as material to be processed and released.
- I humbly ask my Higher Power to remove my shortcomings.
- I release my ancient hurts and grudges.
- I set myself free from negative energy.
- I resolve all in love.
- I release myself from _____.
- I forgive myself for the pain I have felt.

- I thank myself and set myself free.
- I resolve what has limited me in love.
- I release you, _____, to your own good.
- I forgive myself for the pain I have felt regarding you.
- I thank you for these lessons and set you free.
- I resolve what has been between us in love.

ELEVEN

The Doormat Doesn't Live Here Anymore

Listen now to that emerging voice within,
Stilled from years of lying on the floor,
Heard at last above the ceaseless din
Saying "Hasten child, come through the door."
Changing generational patterns for women and men,
The Doormat doesn't live here anymore.

Lynne Namka

Getting Up Off The Floor

How are you doing by now? Have you found yourself time and again in these pages? Are you overwhelmed by all that you need to learn and change? You needn't be. Growth, like everything else, is achieved one step at a time. As the ancient philosopher said, "A journey of a thousand miles starts with a single step." The way to recovery is to learn the skills necessary for mature relationships. You will find your own unique way. The important thing is to begin.

Let's repeat some of the basics of this book. Here are some snappy one-liners to tuck away in your brain to pull out, dust off and use when you feel a surge of Doormat behavior about to emerge:

1. Responsibility is understanding that you have put yourself in the situation out of your beliefs and choices, and that you can take yourself out of the situation when you discover new beliefs and make new choices.
2. Sometimes it is necessary to close the open hand out of love.
3. Redefine your boundaries of helping to benefit both you and the other person.
4. When you are responsible only for your own stuff, the other person has more choices.
5. Sometimes the best thing you can do for another person is to say no.
6. The cleanest response is to take care of me and let you take care of you.
7. Love is caring enough to take the sometimes painful responsibility of letting the other person be who they are.
8. Listen to what you know instead of what you fear.
9. When you are in touch with your integrity and tune in to your Inner Wisdom, you make good choices on your behalf.

The First Generation

For the first time in the history of the world, there are techniques and tools to assist those caught in chemical, drug, sexual and relationship addictions. Those of us who are making these vast changes in our lives by learning more about ourselves are the First Generation. We are the first generation to come forth from those dysfunctional families to learn wholeness and personal power. Information from the research and clinical programs in the fields of psychology, chemical dependency and family systems theory is reaching the public. It is exciting to be living in a time where there are resources to break into patterns of generational incest, alcoholism, domination and co-dependency.

There are self-help groups such as Al-Anon and Adult Children of Alcoholics that focus on co-dependency. Alcoholics Anonymous, Gamblers Anonymous, Narcotics Anonymous, Overeaters Anonymous and Emotions Anonymous provide inpatient and outpatient treatment programs. The 12-Step programs are helping numbers of people recover from their addictions while developing that deep sense of spirituality and a knowledge of the Inner Self. Many local chapters of the National Association for Children of Alcoholics have been established so that men and women can look at their patterns of co-dependency. Workshops are being offered by individuals who have found ways to work through their own recovery process. If your community does not have a self-help group, start one based on this book. People supporting people — that is what this age is about.

The help is there. We of this First Generation can take advantage of the expanded knowledge and techniques to bring about an end to the pain that has been passed from parent to child. We all are being given the opportunity to participate in our own unique healing.

You will need help along the way. Co-dependency is a pervasive, progressive problem. Do not delude yourself that you can accomplish this great task of recovery all by yourself. The process of becoming yourself is greatly facilitated by those who have gone before you and are accomplishing their own healing process. Place yourself with people who can believe in you and see the true beauty that is within you. The best gift that you can give yourself in times of loneliness and low self-esteem is to allow someone to gift you by believing in you and by confirming that inner strength you possess until the time you firmly know this to be true.

Therapy is available for those who learn best from the individual approach or for those who have gone through groups but still need to uncover individual issues that are unresolved from childhood.

You now have some understanding about the co-dependency syndrome, your past patterns of ineffectiveness and your unique needs. You are ready to make the decision to bring balance into your life. Resolve will develop as you gather together the forces within you that firmly state, "I have carried out this co-dependent behavior long enough. I don't have to do this anymore!" The knowledge that you have about your life, and the approaches and methods by which you learn best will help you discover which avenues lead the way on the road to recovery. You may need a combination of different therapeutic approaches or different methods in the different phases of your recovery process. Take positive action to develop new skills by choosing, according to your need, from among the following:

- Reading books about addiction, co-dependency, communication skills and spirituality
- Self-help and support groups
- Experiential workshops
- Relaxation techniques
- Meditation
- Visualization
- Developing positive addictions
- Communication training
- Assertiveness training
- Body work, massage and Rolfing
- Rebirthing and polytrophic breathing

- Individual therapy
- Outpatient or inpatient treatment programs at residential facilities
- Music, art, poetry and journal writing

Choose a therapist, self-help group or a treatment plan that is knowledgeable, positive and optimistic. Take your time in choosing the right person or program for you. Shop around and ask questions about their training, approach, amount of time needed and fee structure. Listen for hidden messages of control and domination on the part of the counselor or therapist as you discuss your needs. Always choose a therapist or group who has fewer psychological problems than you do and is at a higher level of consciousness. Unskilled therapists or facilitators can actually prevent you from getting in touch with your feelings and can create more dependency by projecting their unmet power needs on you. If you are already in therapy and are not experiencing continual growth, then it may be that you have learned all there is to learn from that particular person. Some therapists are right for a certain period of your life and can help you with certain issues, but then you may outgrow them.

You may need a combination of different types of treatment. In the time frame of your recovery, different methods may be better for you at different periods. Each step along the way is a part of the process or recovery, and has its own needs. Choose someone with whom you will really be willing to know yourself when you are with them. That is the test of an excellent therapist or group experience — you are encouraged to really know and celebrate who you are. Here is a checklist of some of the qualities in therapists or groups that will facilitate your growth:

_____ Have gone or are going through a similar type growth process regarding addictions

_____ Know their own addictions and have learned to truly take care of themselves

_____ Truly understand the addictive process because of training and life experiences

_____ Are trained in a family systems approach to deal with both past and present influences on behavior

_____ Allow you to do 75 percent of the talking during the session

_____ Use an experiential, getting-in-touch-with-your-feelings approach rather than intellectualizing or lecturing

_____ Use techniques of processing your issues rather than just having you tell your life story and then giving advice

_____ Use a supportive, understanding approach instead of attempting to control, dominate or manipulate you

_____ Strengthen your resources so that you can better make decisions and insist that you make them, giving you information and alternatives instead of telling you what to do

_____ Use support instead of anger or belittling when you do not follow through on a treatment goal

_____ Bring your shortcomings and issues to you in a confrontive but loving way rather than ignoring them

_____ Have a realistic expectation of what can be accomplished and can help you set goals to bring it about

_____ Are always cognizant of your needs and do not use you to meet their sexual, emotional or social needs

_____ Have worked through their own co-dependency needs so that they do not need to rescue or fix you

_____ Use methods to help you learn your own power rather than keeping you dependent on them

The Courage To Be

All of your life you have been a doer. You have spent your energy doing for, rescuing and taking care of others. You may have been a high achiever continually working on projects. Your co-dependency behavior has been a way you have put off looking at your own problems and finding your True Self. In the misguided pursuit of happiness by pleasing others and keeping busy, you have not learned to be happy. Now you are faced with a different challenge. The question now is, "To do or to be?" This is not a selfish question. The process of finding out who you are will bring you to a place where those around you will also benefit from your growth. Being yourself is the greatest challenge you will ever face. To be truly open now at this period of your life requires discipline. Dedicating your life to being — finding out who you are and how you can be happy — requires total self-honesty. The openness to becoming oneself requires continual acts of courage. Now is the time for you to draw on your Inner Wisdom to guide you in this search for self.

Do not put off getting help by worrying about the cost. Some people develop a belief that they do not have the money for treatment. This is a false belief. The real issue is not a lack of money but a lack of hope and courage that comes from living a lifetime of believing you are not worthy. You are worth whatever it takes in terms of money or time to bring about this great accomplishment of becoming who you truly are. Think of the cost of obtaining help as an investment in you and your future. It is also an investment for your family and children that pays off in huge dividends. As you grow in maturity, you will model appropriate behavior for others, thus contributing to their learning process. Treatment for co-dependency does not cost — it pays in dividends all around. Tell yourself again and again, "I am worth the cost. Whatever it takes, I am worth it."

The ancient Chinese proverb tells us, "If we do not change our direction, we are likely to end up where we are headed." Develop a plan for changing your Doormat belief systems and behavior, as in the following:

1. Take yourself out to lunch and give yourself a good talking to about what you will do to change the direction you have been headed.
2. Listen to what you are saying. No tuning out — no deaf ears! Listen to what you really need to hear. Address those fears that will try to talk you out of this change process.
3. Know, really know, if this is right for you. Get in touch with your Inner Wisdom and determine what your real longing for becoming whole is. What type of person do you want to be?
4. Resolve to do what is in your best interest by seeking help. Commit to your ideals and goals.
5. Do it! Make it happen. Practice your new skills until they become automatic.

Going Home Again

The process of recovery from co-dependency starts with an identification of the problem and the symptoms. It addresses the unresolved childhood issues of abandonment and unmet needs to heal the memories as you separate yourself from the pain of the past. The recovery process looks at belief systems and communication styles that are not productive and at dysfunctional ways of coping. It continues with developing your own Inner Wisdom, strength and integrity. The process is never easy. But it is an exciting journey as you find out who you are becoming. The honing and fine-tuning of yourself takes you down to your true grain. William Keats, the mystic poet, stated it well when he said, "Not myself goes home to myself."

Finding your own unique identity is the gift that the lessons of co-dependency hold for you. Richard Bach in *Illusions, Confessions Of A Reluctant Messiah* relates, "There is no such thing as a problem without a gift for you in its hands. You seek problems because you need their gifts." What you are seeking in this process of recovery is the gift of your own True Self and the love that is deep within you. This too is your "own" coming home to you. What we experience as loss and pain, such as illness, divorce or death, is simply a temporary developmental disorganization that presents us with its own unique gifts.

"All healing is a release from the past," *A Course In Miracles* states. The means to achieve this release is through forgiveness. Forgiveness as a healing process has been taught by the scriptures of the major world religions. To forgive means simply to give up something. Giving up all beliefs and thoughts that separate you from others or yourself through criticism and judgment will help transform your life into one of harmony and joy.

One theme of your life may have been to carry the pain from the past forward and continue the same behavior patterns that act to bring tragedy into the present. You may have separated from your parents physically, but you will not be free from them psychologically until you address those old debts and grievances. Our parents are always part of our being. While it is not always possible to go home again, the ancient ghosts of ill will can be laid to rest. Old hurts revisited can be seen through new lenses of perception.

In many ways we are the motherless or fatherless child still seeking the sources of those unrecognized needs. Yet, at some point we must grow past our parents to become complete. To become whole we must become the parent of our own being. The task is to let go of the sense of loss in childhood, to accept our parents as the imperfect people that they were and give up the expectation of the loving wonderful parent of our dreams who meets all of our unfulfilled needs. We can understand our parents' limitations through the familial and cultural factors that shaped their personalities and styles of parenting. We can learn to understand their shortcomings and learn to relate to them in new ways through the simple act of forgiveness. In the sense that we change our belief systems about what has happened and take away the power that pain has held over us, we can rewrite the past. Thus, in rewriting the past we can create our own bright future. One way to accomplish this is to go back and honor the little child that we once were.

Loving That Little Child Of Your Past

You can give in to that child of your past who did not feel loved in the right way. This visual imagery exercise will enable you to reassure that child that he is perfect and worthy of love in every way.

Close your eyes and clear your mind of everyday matters. Breathe deeply from your diaphragm as you allow yourself to slip back in time. Count backward in terms of years that you have been on earth and allow yourself to see glimpses of yourself at the different ages. Smile gently at these former versions of yourself. Be in touch with those decisions you have made that proved unfruitful when you were only trying to seek love. Honor these decisions as the best you could do at the time and gently release them.

Continue counting backward through your teenage years. Notice the awkward feelings in your body as you move back in time remembering who you were. Do not get stuck in any painful memory as you breathe and count backward. Continue until you have a sense of how old that little child was when it knew that it was not loved. Place that child in a familiar setting that was comfortable. See the scenery surrounding it. Be aware of the memories, sensations and feelings in the child's body.

How does the child feel? _____

What event(s) brought about these feelings? _____
Why does that little child feel betrayed? In what way was it not loved enough

or in the wrong way? _____

_____

How does the child feel about what it is feeling? _____
Describe any element of guilt or shame that needs to be recognized at this

time. _____

What does that little child want to do with these feelings? _____

_____

Be in touch with the longing of the child. What does your little child want?

_____

Go now to your Adult Self. Visualize yourself standing straight and tall being very wise and knowing. Know that you have had a lifetime to learn about real loving and making better choices. The little child made choices based only on what it knew at that time. As your Adult Self, draw from your vast resources of experiences and knowing. Be in touch with your wholeness and your ability to heal yourself. Call the name of that healer part of yourself to help you. Ask your Higher Power to assist you in this important undertaking of loving that little child that you once were.

See your little child self and your adult, loving self standing facing each other. Your Adult Self knows what that part of yourself from your past needs.

Ask the little child what it needs to hear from your Adult Self. _____

_____

Ask it what it needs to feel loved and whole. _____

_____

Tell it of your wisdom and what you have learned over the years. _____

Acknowledge the pain that the child is feeling. _____

Tell the child that it has not been easy for you living with pain that those unhappy belief systems have created and that you are learning to create more positive ways of thinking. _____

Tell it of your strength and how you have survived despite the traumas that you have experienced. Share your strength with that child. _____

Tell it of the power that it can learn in the future to help deal with those feelings of unworthiness and shame. _____

Reassure it that it is worthwhile and lovable. _____

Ask the child what it needs to know at this point. _____

See the child reach out its arms to you. It wants to be loved and to know, really know that it is truly lovable. Take that child up in your Adult Self arms and give it the comfort that it has been seeking all of these years. Hold it and caress it and tell it of its beauty and wholeness. _____

Give that child your unconditional love. Tell it all that you know about true loving. _____

Ask your child if there is anything else that it needs. _____

Reassure the little child that you can always draw from your wisdom to give it what it needs. You can share what you know to replace its inner fears about not being lovable. Visualize both of you standing straight and tall now as you silently acknowledge each other's ability to love and be loved.

As you focus on the process of forgiveness, incidents that have harbored grudges and grievances that you had forgotten will surface out of your subconscious mind asking for release. When you start the process of recovery, past anger and guilt will come tap, tap, tapping on the everyday consciousness, crying for resolution. This is one of the Steps in the 12-Step program — to make amends to those individuals in your life who have been in conflict with you. As you release each incident, peace and harmony come rushing in to fill up that space that was formerly occupied by negative energy. As old grudges and resentments fall away, you become more free and creative.

The process of forgiving moves from an intellectual to an emotional level; it moves from the head down into the heart or gut. We may know something cognitively before we really accept it on a gut level. Exercises, such as the ones presented in this book and those given in experiential workshops and therapy, will help move the knowing down from your mind to your loving center of the heart. The gravity of a conflictual issue and your deep yearning to find peace can pull it down to an experiential level where it can be resolved.

Honoring The Resistant Part Of You

You may feel resistance at forgiving someone or yourself as old habits are sometimes challenging to break. Know that resistance is only a part of who you are. Resistance may bubble up as the "Yes, yes, yes, I know, but . . . ." Honor this part of you that wants to keep you safe in its own particular way. Your boycott on this forgiveness issue is your way of hanging on to the familiar — what you know and have practiced all these years. Resistance is like denial; it is a way of keeping you safe by avoiding taking in new information. It merely means that this is an important issue for you. When you work with it instead of fighting it, it will stand aside to let you accomplish what you need to do.

Thank the resistance and accept it as just another part of you. What do you

call your stubborn part? _____

_____

Give a statement of welcome to that part of you that doesn't want to change.

_____

Remember the saying, "What you resist, persists." Don't resist the resistance! That only makes it more stubborn and entrenched. Tell your resistance that

you do not intend to force it or fight it. _____

_____

Honor it and talk to it about the gift that it has held for you over the years. Resistance is not to be overcome, but it is to be understood. What is the

message behind the opposition? _____

_____

Ask your resistance what you could do for it. Ask it what it needs to feel

whole and integrated with the rest of the parts of your personality. _____

_____

Forgiveness is a three-fold issue — forgiveness of other people, forgiveness of yourself and forgiveness of God if there are feelings that divine intervention brought about trauma and misfortune in life. For some women who have closely identified with the Goddess, there may be an additional need to forgive that masculine sense of God from whom you feel separation. You may need to forgive an institution, such as a former church or school, where you feel you were not treated well.

Any time you feel conflict or anger in your daily life, there is a forgiveness issue underneath, crying for resolution. Call on your Higher Self to assist you in areas that do not resolve easily. Know the pain you experience by making it conscious. Honor it, then release it by letting go of the expectations that you have set up around that pain.

If necessary, work through the resistant issues in therapy and workshops designed to help you learn who you truly are — someone who is connected to the whole universe. Remember there is no need for separation from anything — not from others, from God or from the disjointed parts of yourself. As you practice the daily acts of forgiveness for past and present transgressions, you will become more integrated with yourself.

Forgive, Forgive And Forgive Some More

Find the name that is the healer part of yourself. It is the part of you that

knows forgiveness and wants you to be whole and happy. _____

_____

This is the part that moves past wanting to be right and justified and moves into that deep yearning to be free. What has been your message to yourself about forgiveness? Is it all right for you to forgive others or yourself? Do you

see the act of forgiving as a weakness? _____

_____

If you were forced as a child to say, "I'm sorry," when you were angry, you may have picked up some mixed messages about forgiveness. If so, turn this confusion over to your Higher Power and ask for resolution. Meditate on the phrase, "Do I want to hold on or do I want peace of mind?"

Look deeply into the hurts and betrayals of your past and present life that have left the scars of grudges on you. Let issues gently come to the surface of your mind so that you can be reminded of situations waiting to be released and resolved through love. Do not spend time and negative energy on each one. Simply let all of them come forth to be written down.

Be specific in your descriptions using the formula of "When _____

did _____, I felt . . ." _____.

_____

_____

_____

_____

_____

Fully allow yourself to feel the emotions of anger and fear that you have been harboring in each of the above situations. Say silently to each person involved, "For all errors that you have committed, whether on purpose or by accident, that have resulted in my choosing to feel pain, I release you. In doing so, I release myself from the pain." When an issue is released, you may experience tears, feel a shift in your body or feel lighter. Some issues and people will be released easily. Others may take more time and work.

Now list all the people both past and present that you would like to forgive you. Feel the guilt or shame that you may have retained from these unresolved areas of your life. Be specific as to what your transgression was regarding each incident.

_____

_____

_____

_____

_____

_____

Say to the person in your mind, "I fully allow you to forgive me for my part in this circumstance." Close your eyes and picture the people extending their hands in forgiveness. You may choose to talk to some of these people about what you are doing.

Now center in on the areas where you are disappointed with yourself. Think of the negative adjectives that you call yourself — these are areas in which the perfectionistic part of yourself is still expressing dissatisfaction. Write down all of your failures and mistakes that you continue to feel regret over, and the unrealistic expectations that you have about yourself.

_____

_____

_____

_____

_____

_____

Record the following self-release statements on a cassette recorder and use as a daily meditation. Record these words in a slow, dreamy rhythm that is consistent with a slowed breathing pattern. Allow enough time after each statement on the tape for you to repeat the statement to yourself a second time. This slow-paced technique will help keep your mind on the meditation as you hear the statement, breathe in and out, and then repeat the statement to yourself while breathing in and out. Play the tape at the beginning and end of the day to assist your process of forgiveness.

"I prepare now to place myself in a loving consciousness where I can release that which no longer fits for me. I go deeper and deeper into total relaxation. I close my eyes and breathe deeply as I count backward from twenty to one. (Add the numbers here, breathing deeply as you say each one.) I go to a deep, deep place of Inner Wisdom. I allow all that is growth-producing within me to come forth and assist me. I become more and more relaxed.

"I speak now from my heart of hearts. I ask my Higher Self to join me in this endeavor. I am responsible for what I experience. I ask for forgiveness from myself, from others, from God and from the universe. I ask to erase the hurtful memories. I release myself from unnecessary power struggles. I release myself from my addiction to pain. I let go of my unrealistic expectations I have held for others. I disengage from the pain I have unnecessarily carried for another person in his struggle. I allow release from unrealistic expectations that I have for myself. I forgive myself for those situations where I felt failure. I let go of my need for perfectionism.

"I participate fully in my own recovery. I see the rightness in my new ways of thinking that are gentle and loving. I replace old, worn-out belief systems with new productive ones. I am whole and seek only that which is beneficial for me. I honor me for who I am. I honor others for who they are. I affirm the healing qualities of forgiveness. I allow forgiveness to surge through me for my release from self-doubt and pain. I now invite any situation that requires release to gently come to my mind . . . . (Turn off the tape recorder at this time and work through the issue.)

"I thank myself for allowing these healing moments. I thank my Higher Self for helping me see this concern in a new way. I honor my process of release. I celebrate my choices of health and wholeness. I am whole and free."

If you find you need more work in forgiving yourself and others, you might consider joining a study group in *A Course In Miracles.*

Symptoms Of Inner Peace

How do you know that you are gaining in growth and wisdom? Working through your co-dependency issues will bring about different ways of perceiving and relating to others. One of the most important goals in life is to achieve peace of mind so that things that used to bother you have no meaning.

Saisha Davis gives the following explanation to describe how you will know you are on the right road to Inner Peace.

> *Watch for signs of Peace. The hearts of a great many have already been exposed to it and it seems likely that we could find our society experiencing it in epidemic proportions. Some signs and symptoms of Inner Peace follow:*
> *1. Tendency to think and act spontaneously rather than from fear*
> *2. An unmistakable ability to enjoy each moment*
> *3. Loss of interest in judging other people*
> *4. Loss of interest in judging self*
> *5. Loss of interest in interpreting the actions of others*

6. *Loss of interest in conflict*
7. *Loss of ability to worry (a very serious symptom)*
8. *Frequent, overwhelming episodes of appreciation*
9. *Contented feelings of connectedness with others and with nature*
10. *Frequent attacks of smiling through the eyes and from the heart*
11. *Increasing tendency to let things happen rather than make them happen*
12. *Increased susceptibility to love extended by others as well as the uncontrollable urge to extend it*

If you have all or even most of the above symptoms, please be advised that your condition may be too far advanced to turn back. If you are exposed to anyone exhibiting several of these symptoms, remain exposed at your own risk. This condition of Inner Peace is likely well into its infectious stage. Be forewarned.

This time in which we live is a quickening time and a hastening time, as those of us in the First Generation move through our process. We are going through changes more rapidly than any time in history. We are being presented with lesson after lesson in rapid succession so that we can further participate in self-growth. It has been said by those much wiser than ourselves that we are being pulled by our own future — we are pulled by whom we are becoming.

Your future — that person you are to become — is pulling you with the assistance of your Higher Self. You are being shown the way in a step-by-step fashion. If you are sincere in your journey, there are no missteps. Your so-called mistakes only provide the opportunity for looking at new ways to grow. There is only perfection coming forth for you if you make the choice for continued growth.

What you are learning is about the meaning of love. That little child that you were did not experience true loving. After all, what is merely a statement of love and what is true loving? What you knew were mere words of how you should love by giving yourself away. The subtle expectation that you were to be an adult at all times in your family, even when you were small, is not true loving. You have spent your whole life saying, "Love me, love me, I just want to be loved." You have learned patterns of appeasing and placating as a way of trying to gain that love. You may have grown up with the lie that love is earned by being nice to people. That is conditional love based on fear and feelings of lack in both the recipient and giver.

Love is not passion although passion is often present in love. Co-dependent behavior seeks the euphoria and emotionality that is sometimes confused with true loving. Love is a state of being, not a supercharged emotion that is tainted with possession and pain. "Falling in love" can become a trap that requires an object (the beloved) to obtain happiness. Nonjudgmental love of yourself and others can become a way of being and a way of living through the understanding of your Higher Self. Being is a condition of your lovingness that is sufficient unto itself. It is independent of an object. Your own being is a most wondrous experience. Become a being in love and you can love without the fear of loss. Ask yourself the age-old question, "What is the quality of your loving?" Work with your Higher Power to create a more loving reality for yourself.

Now you are being given a second chance to learn who you are and participate in the joyous expression of loving. Your little child who wasn't loved enough in the right way is learning to stop trying to obtain love from your parents, who for reasons of their own, could not give it. You are being given the opportunity to experience and express genuine loving that offers a respite from the confusion and conflict you have experienced all your life. You also are being given the opportunity to grow through your love experiences. Finally, you are learning that true loving is purity of mind, heart and deep humility.

You are learning to love without being unduly attached to that object of your love. Mature love is the opposite of interpersonal addiction. It is a mutual recognition of both partners' right to grow and expand. True loving is equally valuing self and others, and respecting the boundaries and integrity of one another. It is achieved when the partners are complete within themselves having a whole, separate identity, yet desiring a union with each other with the condition of preserving the integrity of both.

You are learning to put your energy into respecting and loving yourself as well as others. This is your heritage. Your divine child is awakening within. Your choice now is to step forward and claim what is rightfully yours. You are the guardian of the beauty, wholeness and sacredness within you that constitutes your true loving.

Opening Of The Heart

Close your eyes and allow yourself to drift into a state of relaxation and peace. Permit yourself to access a deeper place of consciousness than you have ever achieved before. Count backward as you visualize transcending a staircase that takes you to the deep regions of the heart. Feel the energy in your personal power that is all loving and giving based on mutual respect for yourself and others. Draw energy, love and light from the universe, allowing it to swirl through your body and accumulate in your heart center.

Perceive how the heart center beats, drawing from the swirling energy and giving you life. Notice your personal rhythm that vibrates in synchronicity with the rhythm of the universe. Breathe in accordance with the natural pulse of the universe. Observe how the pulse of life flows through your veins giving you further empowerment. Breathe in and out knowing that you bring in light and love to further strengthen your body. The light adds to your sense of being alive and full of zest.

See how your heart is opening up. See how it swells with gratitude for all you are learning. The love and light stream in adding to the expansion of your heart center. You feel completely relaxed and resonate in harmony with all who are around you. You notice that you have no need to be judgmental about the actions of others. There is nothing to do about the sufferings of others because you view them in a different way. You feel warm and happy in allowing them the opportunity for growth without your unnecessary intervention. You feel pleased with this decision. This new delicious sense of well-being is so enjoyable that you decide to keep it with you at all times.

Your heart center continues to throb and expand in your understanding that you are perfect. In your opening to love, you are accepting your divinity. You are wonderfully perfect even in your imperfections and mistakes of the moment. You celebrate your perfection.

❧ BIBLIOGRAPHY ❧

A Course In Miracles. Farmingdale, NY: Foundation For Inner Peace, 1975.

Adler, A., **Understanding Human Nature**. London: Allen & Unwin, 1928.

Bach, R., **Illusions. Confessions of a Reluctant Messiah**. New York: Delacorte Press, 1977.

Bettelheim, B., **The Empty Fortress: Infantile Autism and the Birth of the Self**. New York: Free Press, 1967.

Black, C., Bucky, S., and Wilder-Padilla, S., "The interpersonal and emotional consequences of being an adult child of an alcoholic." *International Journal of the Addictions*, Vol. 21 (2), 1986.

Booth, L., **Spirituality And Recovery: Walking On Water**. Deerfield Beach, FL: Health Communications, 1985.

Castaneda, C., **The Fire From Within**. New York: Simon & Shuster, 1984.

Diagnostic and Statistical Manual of Mental Disorders. Third Edition Revised., Washington, DC: American Psychiatric Association, 1987.

Glasser, W., **Positive Addictions**. New York: Harper & Row, 1976.

Erikson, E., **Childhood and Society**. New York: W.W. Norton, 1950.

Field, R., **The Invisible Way**. San Francisco: Harper & Row, 1979.

Fromm, E., **The Art of Loving**. New York: Harper & Row.

Gibran, K., **The Prophet**. New York: Alfred Knopf, 1923.

Hazen, C., and Shaver, P. "Love Conceptualized as an Attachment Process," *Journal of Personality and Social Psychology*, 52, 1978.

Horney, K., **Neurotic Personality of Our Times**. New York: W.W. Norton, 1937.

Howard, V., **The Powers Of Your Supermind**. New York: Parker Publishers, 1967.

Jung, C.G., **Man and His Symbols**. New York: Doubleday, 1976.

Kaplan, S., **Jungian-Senoi Dreamwork Manual**. Journey Press, 1980.

Leonard, G. **The Silent Pulse**. New York: E.P. Dutton, 1978.

Menaker, E., "Masochism: a defense reaction of the ego," *Psychoanalytic Quarterly,* 22, 205-222, 1953.

Menaker, E., **Masochism and the Emergent Ego**, New York: Human Sciences Press, 1979.

Milkman, H., and Sunderwirth, S., **Craving for Ecstasy. The Consciousness and Chemistry of Escape**. Lexington, MA: Lexington Books, 1981.

Prigogine, I., and Stengers, I., **Order Out of Chaos: Man's New Dialogue With Nature**. New York: Bantam Books, 1984.

Satir, V., **Conjoint Family Therapy**. Palo Alto, CA: Science and Behavior Books, 1964.

Satir, V., **Peoplemaking**. Palo Alto, CA: Science and Behavior Books, 1972.

Satir, V., **Self-Esteem**, Milbrae, CA: Celestial Arts, 1976.

Satir, V., **Making Contact**. Milbrae, CA: Celestial Arts, 1976.

Satir, V., **Your Many Faces**. Milbrae, CA: Celestial Arts, 1978.

Seligman, M., **Helplessness: On Depression, Development and Death**. San Francisco: Freeman, 1975.

Small, J., **Transformers, The Therapists of the Future**. Marina del Rey, CA: Vross, 1982.

Tzu, Lao, **Tae te Ching**. New York: Viking Penguin, 1963. D. Lau, translator.

Made in the USA
Middletown, DE
03 September 2015